Marilyn Monroe

Marilyn Monroe

A LIFE ON FILM

introduction by **DAVID ROBINSON**

compiled and edited by **JOHN KOBAL**

HAMLYN

London · New York · Sydney · Toronto

For my parents, whom I deeply
love, this book . . . J.K.

Published by
The Hamlyn Publishing Group Limited
London · New York · Sydney · Toronto
Astronaut House, Feltham, Middlesex, England

ISBN 0 600 36172 1

Designed by Dodd and Dodd
Printed in Great Britain by
Jarrold and Sons Limited, Norwich

CONTENTS

'Marilyn', wrote Edward Wagenknecht, 'played the best game with the worst hand of anybody I knew.' She inherited a distinctly unpromising patrimony. She never even knew who her father was. He might have been a mechanic called Mortensen, or a man called Gifford who worked at Consolidated Film Industries where Marilyn's mother was a negative cutter, or he might have been a Mr Baker who was the father of her elder brother and sister. Her maternal grandparents were both ultimately committed to mental institutions; her mother, whose photographs show her to have been a woman of considerable beauty, was to spend most of her life in and out of mental hospitals. An uncle committed suicide.

Parental deprivations and childhood penury, oddly enough, are misfortunes that Hollywood's greatest stars have in common. Chaplin's father abandoned the family when Charles was one; Fairbanks' when the future star was four. Mary Pickford's father died when she was four, Valentino's when he was eleven, Garbo's when she was thirteen. Like Marilyn, Chaplin was early deprived of maternal affection by his mother's retreat into madness. Marilyn spent two years in the Los Angeles Orphan Home and the rest of her childhood and adolescence in a series of foster homes. In later years she claimed to have been raped at nine by a boarder in one of these houses; but that may have been a fantasy of her later life, when the person and the role often became confused.

The last of her guardians encouraged her to marry, when she was just sixteen years and three weeks, a 22-year-old neighbour, an aircraft worker who was soon to be drafted into the Marines. Again it is interesting to remark a kind of pattern in the formation of stars: Mae West, Jean Harlow, Rita Hayworth, Betty Grable, Jane Russell, Jayne Mansfield and Raquel Welch were other Hollywood sex-symbols who in private life found themselves physically ripe for marriage before the age of seventeen.

Mae West

Jean Harlow

Betty Grable

What made Marilyn Monroe different from practically all the other great stars was that she was a child of Hollywood, born and reared in the movie capital. She was born on June 1, 1926 in the Los Angeles General Hospital and registered as Norma Jeane Mortensen. (The surname was evidently speculative: the 'e' on Jeane was never used again.) The streets she knew as a child housed the studios, then in their glory, and were trodden by the stars. Even in the orphanage, it is said, her bedroom window looked directly on to the neon sign of RKO.

She was born into Coolidge's American miracle, which in three years more was to end in ruin, but for the moment had accustomed the American people to confidence in material plenty, in cars and radios, ice boxes and women's emancipation, the Charleston and jazz babies, petting parties and Dancing Mothers, speakeasies and gang warfare. Around the time of her birth Dempsey was fighting Tunney; Babe Ruth, Bobby Jones and Red Grange were the idols of the nation; and Lindbergh was about to make his most celebrated flight. Norma Jean's crazy grandmother was one of Aimée Semple McPherson's most fanatical fans, and the baby was baptized in the evangelist's Temple. Alongside all the other enthusiasms of the age, everyone went to the movies. John Barrymore and Mary Astor had just made *Don Juan*, the first all-synchronized feature; Fairbanks had made *The Black Pirate* in colour; Keaton *The General*; Garbo *The Torrent*. Lillian Gish and John Gilbert appeared in King Vidor's *La Bohème*. Norma Talmadge, in honour of whom the child Norma Jean was named, had just made *Kiki*, with Ronald Colman. When Norma Jean was six weeks old, Rudolph Valentino died; and the unprecedented demonstrations at his lying-in-state marked the apogee of America's deification of the mute idols of the screen.

When she was herself a star, Marilyn Monroe explained

Rita Hayworth

Marilyn, hair set Gilda fashion by Helen Hunt

Lana Turner

Marilyn Monroe, *The Asphalt Jungle*

why she would never permit 'ghosted' articles to appear over her name. 'I might never see that article' she told Pete Martin, the *Saturday Evening Post* columnist: 'and it might be okayed by somebody in the studio. This is wrong, because when I was a little girl I read signed stories in fan magazines and I believed every word the stars said in them. Then I'd try to model my life after the lives of the stars I read about. If I'm going to have that kind of influence, I want to be sure it's because of something I've actually read or written.' She also told Martin that she 'used to play act all the time. For one thing, it meant I could live in a more interesting world than the one around me.'

Oddly, however, her biographies and interviews provide little evidence of visits to the cinema, nor indicate at what point her own determination to be in pictures was born. Certainly, a settled determination there must have been, to enable this essentially lonely young girl to survive and persist through the long five years of pushing and rejection, optimism and disappointment, before her first film test and the breakthrough to stardom. The first steps in her career look, in retrospect, casual enough. She was working in an aircraft factory when a visiting photographer taking shots for official propaganda publications, remarked on her photogenic potential. He introduced her to an agent, Emmeline Snively, who groomed her and by 1946 had turned her into a successful pin-up model. In one month of that year she appeared on the covers of five magazines. After a smart publicity stunt invoking the name of Howard Hughes, Miss Snively secured Norma Jean a test with 20th Century Fox, the studio for which the bulk of her subsequent work was to be done. Fox's talent scout, the former actor Ben Lyon, immediately saw possibilities in her but advised her to change her name. Monroe was her grandmother's married name; the Marilyn was Lyon's idea, a tribute to his admiration for an earlier star, Marilyn Miller.

HER IMITATORS

Beverly Michaels
Sheree North
Cleo Moore

Jayne Mansfield
Joy Lansing, Barbara Nichols
Mamie Van Doren

Ben Lyon, Marilyn Monroe. He gave her her name

HER CONTEMPORARIES

Kim Novak

Grace Kelly

Marlon Brando

Elizabeth Taylor

James Dean

Audrey Hepburn

She was given a year's contract at $125 a week, received a measure of grooming, posed for stills which seemed to appeal satisfactorily to the press, and worked in a couple of films. Her single line in *Scudda Hoo! Scudda Hay!* was cut though it is said to turn up again in some television versions. In *Dangerous Years* she had a bit part as a confused adolescent; but her contract was not renewed at the end of the year. It is interesting that although she went back to modelling to make a living, she continued to keep up with the classes at the Actor's Lab, for which the studio had enrolled her. Through a combination of the influence of Nicholas Schenck, Harry Cohn, the redoubtable head of Columbia, and Fred Karger, the film's dance director – all three, it seemed, personal admirers – she was given her first featured role in a forgotten Columbia musical, *Ladies of the Chorus* (1948). She also acquired at this time, in Natasha Lytess, a studio drama coach, the first of the series of mentors and confidants who were as necessary to her morale as they were trying to the studios and film-makers with whom she worked.

She seemed to move without intending unkindness from protector to protector at this stage of her career. The agent Johnny Hyde, more than thirty years her senior, fell in love with her; and before he died had firmly launched her career by getting her small but showy parts in the Marx Brothers comedy *Love Happy*; and in *The Asphalt Jungle*, directed by John Huston, who was also to direct her last finished film. After the impact of her brief appearance in this film as the mistress of an ageing gangster (Louis Calhern) her parts got bigger and bigger. *All About Eve* contains one of the earliest autobiographical echoes, as George Sanders sends her wiggling off in the direction of Gregory Ratoff, with the admonition: 'He's a big producer. Go do yourself a bit of good.' The film also contains one of the first authentic Monroisms, ripostes so deceptively artless that they seem like accidents. 'You know Miss Caswell, of course?' asks

Marilyn Monroe, Marlon Brando

Sanders gracefully. 'No' Bette Davis brutally snaps back. 'That' comes back Marilyn with sweet and guileless logic, 'is because we never met.'

The roles that followed confirmed her standing as a sex bomb-shell: accustomed the public to the splendid physique (in those days it sometimes tended to sturdiness), the amazing contours clingingly sheathed, the challenging walk which proclaimed her very real sensuous delight in every bit of her body and its appeal, the fresh skin, large, deep, heavy-lidded eyes, and glittering hair. In *Monkey Business* her spelling caused Charles Coburn to cast his rheumy old eyes over her rear and sigh with happy resignation, 'Well *any* stenographer can take *dictation*.' In *We're not Married* she is half of one of five couples who wake up to find that their marriages are not legally solemnized. Undeterred, she transfers her assets from the Mrs America to the Miss America class of the beauty contest. In *Love Nest* her sexual challenge becomes a narrative motive in the comedy itself, an anecdote about a war veteran whose visiting army buddy turns out, to his wife's chagrin, to be a WAC (Marilyn) instead of a doughboy.

It was, though, Henry Hathaway's somewhat irreverent direction of a torrid melodrama of passion, set against the natural drama of Niagara Falls, which ultimately and permanently confirmed Marilyn as a new sex image, more potent than anything that had gone before. The publicity for *Niagara*, showing Monroe spread sensuously and surrealistically across the top of the roaring falls, celebrated the explosive meeting of the old and the new World Wonders. But particularly *Niagara* immortalized 'The Walk', giving her a scene in which, for 70 feet of film she made her way, away from the camera, walking in high heels across cobble stones. 'The Monroe wiggle' was altogether inadequate as a phrase to describe Marilyn's unique ambulation. It was as if her exhilaration in her being and her body exhilarated every part of her (in *The Misfits* Arthur

Miller had her say, as Roslyn, 'You can hear your skin against your clothes' – a remarkable verbalization of pure sensuousness). As she walks it is an undulation, a percussion, a complex independent dancing of her limbs, of her buttocks and the thighs that seem to have an extra curve (she always gave out her *upper* and her *lower* hip measurement). There was never again such an innocently pagan celebration of the zone till Huston filmed her from behind in *The Misfits* as she zestfully accepted a challenge with a bat and ball.

Just before *Niagara* two films had been striking for the autobiographical illuminations which seemed, much more than with any other star, to characterize her roles. Her appearance in *O Henry's Full House* was brief. In 'The Cop and the Anthem' she plays a lovely young prostitute who is accosted by the shabby-genteel old bum played by Charles Laughton. As he walks away she gazes after him and whispers in poignant disbelief: 'He called me a lady!' Several later Monroe heroines would echo the same craving for respect for their own selves. In *Bus Stop* she says, 'I'm going to marry a man that will have some regard for me apart from all that love and stuff.' In *The Misfits* she exclaims to Montgomery Clift with touching delight: 'You took your hat off to me!'

Already Monroe was established as a sex-pot and comedienne; so that her casting as a psychopath girl in *Don't Bother to Knock* was a surprising miscalculation on the part of the studio, earning some of the worst notices of her career from critics caught off guard by seeing the glamour girl called upon to act. Seen in retrospect it is among her most interesting films, and is far from being her least impressive performance. The study of the deeply disturbed girl with her violent changes of mood and her aimless cruelties towards the child she is supposed to be minding must have been painfully close to her experience; and in one extraordinary speech she blurts out bad memories of foster-parents which are strangely like Marilyn's reported

real-life experiences. Much of her playing is artless; but it is undeniably intense and at moments has striking insights.

The scathing notices however taught the studio their lesson. Monroe did not play a serious dramatic role until her very last completed film. After 1953 and *Niagara* her future seemed set and simple. She had arrived and was defined. In what was to prove the last age of Hollywood superstars in the old manner, the decade that also produced Grace Kelly, Audrey Hepburn, Marlon Brando, James Dean, Kim Novak and the grown-up Elizabeth Taylor, Monroe was supreme. Her achievement in establishing a new sexual type was acknowledged by the wave of imitators which followed in her wake.

Because she was a star, and what she was, she defied imitation, just as she defied comparison with other, earlier stars. She was compared with Clara Bow, with whom it is true she shared some qualities of vitality and the personal difficulties; she was compared with Jean Harlow, with whom she shared the characteristics that she was blonde, an archetypal female symbol and uncompromisingly an American image; she was compared with Mae West, with whom she shared a quality of wit, an ability to be sexually provocative while at the same time parodying all notions of sexuality. She can be compared, but she remains unique and herself. Her uncompromising individuality was already evident in embryo long before she became a star, which is perhaps why Columbia, who had Rita Hayworth, and MGM, where Lana Turner was the reigning goddess, both neglected their chance of Marilyn, while even Fox (with Betty Grable) at first seemed hesitant.

The three years between 1953 and 1956, between *Niagara* and *Bus Stop*, were the most serene and unclouded, comparatively, of her entire professional life (and her professional life seems to have become increasingly more real to her than her personal relationships). She recognized *River of No Return*, in which Otto Preminger rather blatantly

Sophia Loren

EVERY COUNTRY SOUGHT ITS OWN MONROE . . .

Gina Lollobrigida

Martine Carol

Diana Dors

Marilyn Monroe

Anita Ekberg, *Hollywood or Bust*

M★G★M PRESS BOOK

THE WEATHER
By the U. S. Weather Bureau
RAIN. WARMER TONIGHT. RAIN OR SNOW, COLDER TOMORROW.

Vol. CVII No. 3,725 — World Wide Coverage of All News Services ★ ★ ★ ★ ★ Five Cents

STEAL MILLION IN "ASPHALT JUNGLE"

Police Close In On Daring Jewel Gang

Still 1479-57 . . . Mat 3-A

Master-Mind Behind Robbery

Local police are hot on the trail of Doc Erwin Ridenschneider (extreme right), master-mind behind the daring million-dollar jewel robbery at Pelletier and Co. The suicide confession of noted criminal lawyer Alonzo D. Emmerich (left) has also implicated stick-up artist Dix Handley and his girl friend, Doll Conovan, in the robbery. When last seen, Doc was headed for Cleveland, Ohio, in a hired taxi, while police are on the hunt for Handley and his Doll in Kentucky.—Story on page 3.

Still 1479-65 . . . Mat 2-F

Grilled in Jewel Theft

Blonde, baby-faced Angela Phinlay breaks down [——→] after police questioning regarding her wealthy protector, Alonzo D. Emmerich. At first trying to set up a phony alibi for Emmerich by claiming he had been with her at the time the Pelletier jewel robbery took place, Angela finally admits she lied. A few minutes after her confession, Emmerich shot himself with a revolver.—Story on page 3.

concentrated on her sexual attractions, as a mistake. The series of five comedies made in this period, however, revealed to anyone who had eyes to see that rising above the publicity and the pin-up exploitation she had developed into a comedienne gifted enough to reconcile the constants of a dominating star personality with the individual requirements of quite strongly varied roles. The expansion of her technical achievement in these roles is also striking. In *Gentlemen Prefer Blondes*, happily teamed with Jane Russell, she was a funny and touching Lorelei Lee, who could be poignantly silly or huskily seductive. Her comic reactions were very precise and economical, getting a laugh out of the merest gesture or glance. At the same time she could rise to such knockabout farce as the memorable scene in which, having for some reason become stuck (and small wonder) by her hips while climbing through a tiny cabin window, she conceals her predicament by draping a blanket round her neck. She persuades the infant George 'Foghorn' Winslow to provide legs and arms for the strange elongated figure which results and with which a baffled Charles Coburn flirts ineffectively.

In *How to Marry a Millionaire*, teamed again with actresses of a generation preceding her own, Betty Grable and Lauren Bacall, she lightheartedly undermines her own glamour image, playing some kind of offspring of Betty Boop by Mr Magoo, pop-eyed behind enormous spectacles, and without them crashing recklessly into walls. In *There's No Business Like Show Business*, co-starred with formidable veterans like Ethel Merman, Donald O'Connor and Dan Dailey (in whose chorus line she sang in *Ticket to Tomahawk*), she parodies the convention of the stage musical star. In *The Seven Year Itch* she proves the equal of such a veteran comedian as Tom Ewell, and certainly superior to Billy Wilder's rather heavy-handed comedy. In her first appearance in the film, undulating up the stairs in an astonishingly close-fitting gown, she has to say 'My fan's

Exhibitor's campaign book for *Niagara*

caught in the door.' She has made her point and is away, while Wilder is still fumbling with close-ups of her rear.

Arguably the finest performance of this happiest period of her career was the 'chantoose' in Joshua Logan's *Bus Stop*. Bravely and pathetically doing battle with her bar-room audience as she gropes her way in a deep Southern accent through 'That Old Black Magic', stumbling on the kick switch which operates the rudimentary lighting effects of her production, or emerging white, blinking and fearful into the daylight, a creature of the night before, this is a complete, authentic and deeply touching character creation.

In certain respects this was the peak of her career. Already the agonizing difficulties which came more and more to dog her working life had begun to torment her – even more than they did the exasperated directors and studios with whom she worked. She had shown herself an independent spirit; and the studios did not expect that sort of demonstration from their dumb blondes. After *There's No Business Like Show Business* she effected the first of her much-publicized disappearances from the Fox lot, rather than accept scripts which she considered did not suit her (and generally, as events proved, with good reason: she had a near faultless judgment of her material and roles). The studio, knowing where their best interest lay, climbed down and gave her *The Seven Year Itch*. After that film she walked out again and settled in New York. The press joined with the studio in their incomprehension that Monroe should really want to be a serious actress. (The sympathetic Pete Martin ironically called his 1956 interview-portrait 'Will Acting Spoil Marilyn Monroe?')

We shall never, of course, know what would have been her future had she not become involved with the Actors' Studio; with Lee Strasberg who endeavoured to supply some of the cultural and professional education which she felt she lacked; with his wife Paula, who was to succeed Natasha Lytess as Marilyn's drama coach; with Arthur

Miller, who was to become her third husband (a second marriage to the baseball star Joe DiMaggio foundered after less than a year). For Monroe it seemed that even more than self-discovery as an actress, New York was able to offer her the chance to be a person, a woman and an artist in her own right, not merely the sex symbol ('I always thought symbols were things you clashed') and inanimate commercial commodity which the studios sought in her. Her aspirations were admirably fostered when she went to London to star with Laurence Olivier in *The Prince and the Showgirl*, adapted from Terence Rattigan's *The Sleeping Prince*.

The dark years were already claiming her however. Already there was the horrifying dependency on drugs, the capricious moods that were to lead to constant psychiatric attendance and periods in mental clinics which, in view of the heritage of her mother's side of the family, must have been terrifying to her vulnerable spirit. The unpunctuality which had been a joke became a disease and a scourge. Distinguished directors gritted their teeth as she failed to show up on the set for hours and sometimes whole days. She seems till this time to have been irresistibly well-liked by her fellow-workers, but her co-stars now began to dislike her. On Billy Wilder's *Some Like It Hot* Tony Curtis was reported as saying that 'kissing Marilyn Monroe is like kissing Hitler'. 'He only said that', retorted Marilyn with cool insight, 'because I wore prettier dresses than he did.'

Let's Make Love was the most insignificant film of her later career (surprisingly, for it was directed by one of Hollywood's best directors and an old hand with stars, George Cukor) though the filming proved comparatively serene since her morale was lifted by an affair with Yves Montand. Finally she struggled through to *The Misfits*, her last completed film, and perhaps the most fraught and unhappy production in cinema history. Marilyn's marriage to Arthur Miller, who was on hand as the writer of the film, had reached a critical point. She was ill, frequently

incapacitated by narcotics, and hospitalized in the course of a production which dragged on and on. The unit was divided by factions, bitterness, recriminations. Even John Huston's superhuman patience was tried. The film's fatality seemed to outlast the production. Days after the end of filming, Clark Gable died; and three of the other four main stars, Montgomery Clift, Thelma Ritter and Marilyn Monroe herself were dead within a few years.

She was to make one more effort. She owed Fox a last film on her contract, and returned to the studio where her career had begun, to work on *Something's Got to Give*, again directed by Cukor. In the first month of shooting she appeared for work only twelve times. 20th Century Fox fired her and instituted a suit for compensation. Seven weeks later Marilyn Monroe was dead, killed by the drugs that her psychiatrists prodigally handed out to her to help her chronic insomnia (one of a number of aspects which her career had in common with that of an earlier star and sex symbol, Clara Bow). She was alone when she died; and the body which had once been the most desired and desirable in the world lay for days in the Los Angeles Country Morgue, with no friend to claim it.

What was most striking about these last terrible years, however, is that the more tormented Marilyn's private and professional existence became, the more remarkable was her work and appearance on the screen. As Roslyn in *The Misfits*, it is true a certain quality of the earlier years is missing: the gift she had for projecting a unique and incomparable elation appears only fitfully, though it surfaces notably in that exhilarating scene of the contest with the bat and ball. But there are rich compensations. She has become an actress of depth and sublety and power which transcends a role which is not fully realized in the writing. Arthur Miller clearly based Roslyn on a portrait of Marilyn herself; and was perhaps defeated by his own incomprehension of a girl who is finally incomprehensible to

Marilyn poses for the camera between scenes for *Some Like It Hot*

everyone, including herself. Still there are exchanges which are vivid insights into her personality. Clark Gable tells her: 'You're the saddest girl I ever saw.' She replies: 'You're the first man who ever said that. They usually tell me how happy I am.' Again Roslyn's horror, misery and outburst at the inhumanity of the men to the mustangs is based on the extreme, even neurotic and certainly empathetic sensibility which Marilyn showed in respect of animals; and her playing of these scenes is electrifying. Huston shot the film in sequence; in the later scenes, including these, her physical state shows; but the slightly puffy face, the undue hesitancy of the gestures impairs nothing of the performance. In the film's early scenes she was evidently comparatively well and confident. Leaner, refined maturity gave a new beauty to her looks.

In the few brief sequences that were filmed for *Something's Got to Give*, her metamorphosis seems complete. There is no trace now of the eager, round-faced little pin-up of ten years before, in this woman of breathtaking grace and beauty and luminosity and harrowing fragility – ethereal, magical, haunting. In a series of costume tests she walks and walks again (floating now, rather than undulating), moves her head, repeats the action with that hieratic, ritual magic peculiar to mute rushes; and the result is among the most extraordinary material that the screen possesses. The figure has a presence much more real or immediate than can be explained by the physical phenomenon of a light-painted picture. There seems something supernatural, an independent presence, a being.

It is as if Marilyn had finally accomplished some mystical transubstantiation, translation to another element. It is as if, while her sad mother and grandparents had retreated from reality into madness, *she* had sought to protect her too vulnerable spirit by taking it away, giving it sanctuary, finally, in the screen image. Throughout the last years – all the time that she seemed less and less able to communicate

her fears and doubts and anxieties to those around her; as she more and more obscured her consciousness with drugs (years before Billy Wilder had said she 'lived behind a fuzz curtain'); as people in the street came no longer to recognize her in the weary and insignificant girl – the screen image became more real and alive. Gilbert Seldes wrote of Disney that his creations acquired a special spiritual existence because they were drawn, practically, on to the film. Marilyn's image, too, as it appears in *Something's Got to Give*, seems to be created directly on the screen, as if there were no mechanical interposition of cameras and cutting and technicians.

This is all fancy, perhaps: the fact remains that the surviving enchantment of her screen performances is the ability, given to very few of the great personalities of the cinema, to leave on the film the imprint of a real and complete being. Laurence Olivier said of this being that it was able to convey 'naughtiness and innocence at the same time'. She is the most provocative thing that ever was, flaunting all her considerable sexual possibilities, her parted lips at once inviting, taunting, on the edge of laughter; yet at the same time she is as defenceless as a child, with no more nor less than a child's guile. The sexuality is frank and open and unashamed. 'Sex is a part of nature and I get along with nature.' 'Men seem to enjoy me.'

Perhaps her intense sexual allure lay to a large extent in her pure, uninhibited, exhilarated sensuousness. She had a delight – quite distinct from narcissism – in her own being and her body. 'I'm very definitely a woman and I enjoy it.' She wore her dresses two sizes too small, so that she was always conscious, from their clinging, of every part of her physique. ('To wear a dress like that', says an admiring rival in *Niagara*, 'you've got to start laying plans about thirteen'). She liked to look at herself in the mirror; and it was often said with malice that the reason for her incorrigible unpunctuality was her inability to tear herself from

contemplation of her own reflection. Whether she moves or stands or sits, you feel that she is unconsciously feeling and testing and enjoying every limb and every nerve. The nude bathing scene from *Something's Got to Give* is an astonishing moment of exaltation, a solitary act of devotion.

All this was, certainly, natural to her and instinctive. 'I sit down the way I feel.' 'I learned to walk as a baby and I haven't had a lesson since.' 'I use walking to get around.' But the intense joy in her physical being generated an elation which is the irresistible source of her charm, certainly in her earlier roles. In *The Misfits* Gaye tells her: 'You have the gift of life. The rest of us are just looking for a place to hide.' By this time the gift was ebbing, and Marilyn herself had hidden; but still we take this reassurance from her screen presence. Perhaps no one could project so much vitality for so long without finally paying the price, just as Clara Bow had paid for all the spiritual intoxication she had given to the twenties.

But the quality of Marilyn's vitality and exhilaration, certainly in the films of her maturity, was not at all that of a Clara Bow. It was not a brash and bouncing energy. Indeed her special quality is that the joy and elation are always held tremulous on the edge of a precipice of doubt, fear and extreme vulnerability. It is exhilaration always in suspense, fatalistic, trembling lest the next moment it may be wounded. Even when she was at her most sexually aggressive, most triumphant, you never lost sight of the tender, fragile, frightened little thing under the skin, like a Phil May urchin wearing her mother's Sunday boots and hat.

Physically she was obvious, overstated; but her spirit was elusive. Perhaps it was not hard for her to remain so, because her private being defied comprehension – and this was the source of her continuing anguish. There are innumerable records of what she said; few of what she thought. The whole quality of the celebrated Monroe *dicta* is that they too are finally elusive, apparently simple

George Cukor, Marilyn Monroe

Marilyn Monroe, *Something's Got To Give*

and naive, but always suggesting something more or less than the words themselves, some extra significance which is never quite penetrable. Here again the private person ('person' was one of her own favourite words) and the screen image become indistinguishable. From that first worsting of Davis in *All About Eve*, her scripts are never without authentic Monroisms. Did she contribute them or suggest them; or was it simply the way she transformed words by her delivery? Sometimes she seemed to have absorbed and metamorphosed notions from the films. One of her most famous sayings was when she replied, not without mild affront, to a columnist who asked her if she was having an affair with Arthur Miller: 'How could I?' she asked, bewildered; 'He's a married man.' Years earlier, in *The Seven Year Itch* she had used the same logic of innocence when Tom Ewell asked if she was shocked that he was married: of course not, she exclaims: 'I wouldn't be lying on the floor with a married man in the middle of the night if he wasn't married!'

Even if her off-screen sayings were suggested by her roles, the body of epigram and riposte is far too consistent over far too long a period to be entirely attributed to scenarists or press agents (never very witty people). However it came into being, the characteristic mixture of childish sense, acute wit and poetic irrationality are part of the person.

There is so much about her that cannot be explained entirely; and would perhaps never have been explained, even if she had survived to enjoy her person and explore her personality. Though, of course, she *has* survived; or at least that part of her spirit which as time went on was all that really counted for her.

'I'm not interested in money' she told a surprised producer early in her career. 'I just want to be wonderful.' So that despite all the anguish (or because of it) in the end her destiny and her desire came together.

DAVID ROBINSON

PARIS
ATCH
18 AOUT 1962 1 NF
ARILYN
ONROE
vait
dé à Match
jours avant de
ir l'autorisation
PAGES
LIFE
DE GAULLE'S TOUGH
HE WRITES ABOUT EISE
CHURCHILL, F.D.R., ST
CELEBS LEAP FOR CA
LIFE
WHAT REALLY KILLED
MARILYN
by Clare Boothe Luce
yn Monroe eight years
e her suicide
AUGUST 7 · 1964 · 25¢
NEUE
JLLUSTRIERTE
TIME
ATLANTIC EDITION
Marilyn Monro

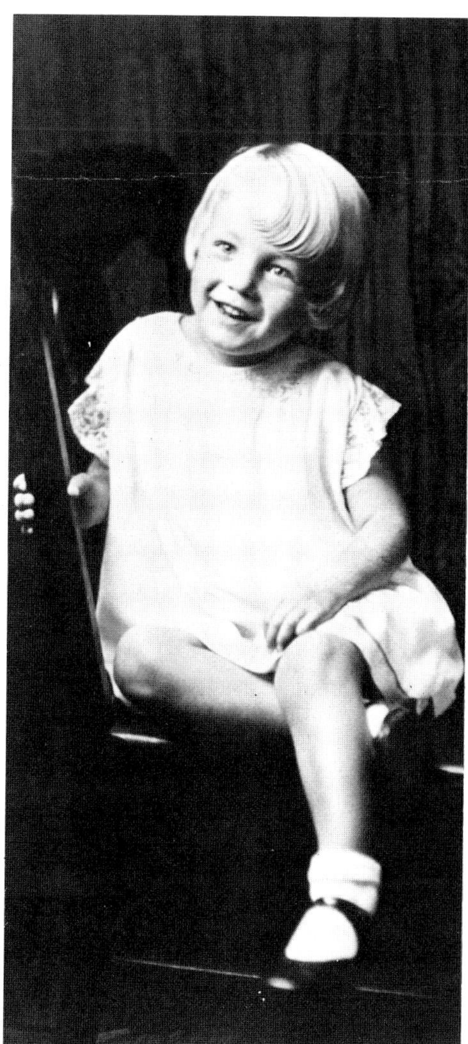

Marilyn at five years old

BEFORE HOLLYWOOD CARED . . .

Marilyn in 1945

Norma Jean Baker, who grew up in orphanages and foster homes when her mother was taken away to the State Mental Hospital for recurring losses of sanity, was like millions of other unhappy kids, though her background gave her a head start. She had an all-consuming dream that would solve all other problems: Get into movies! Become a star! Be loved – as she herself loved the stars she went to see. Norma Jean was a chronic movie addict, and being born and brought up in and around Los Angeles fed the dream.

Marilyn, an official portrait for *All About Eve*

Marilyn – 1950 leg art

What set Norma Jean apart from the millions and led to her metamorphosis into Marilyn Monroe, was her determination to make her fantasy life into reality. Her body was to become her fortune and she showed it off in tight sweaters and skirts. Modelling followed as a matter of course. So did marriage. But by the time she had become a starlet in ermine bikinis, she was single again.

A 1948 publicity shot for *Love Happy*

Robert Karnes, Colleen Townsend, Marilyn Monroe in a scene cut from *Scudda Hoo! Scudda Hay!*

The step from cover girl to starlet is not a big one. She made her first appearance in a rural comedy with the unlikely title of *Scudda Hoo! Scudda Hay!*, rowing in a canoe with fellow hopeful Colleen Townsend. Their scenes had been cut from the film when it was released early in 1948, shortly after she had already been seen in a small role in another film, *Dangerous Years*. Both films were made during her short term contract to 20th Century Fox, the studio whose greatest star she was to become a few years later.

Marilyn between Dickie Moore and Scotty Beckett in *Dangerous Years*

SMW-11-30

Columbia Pictures, home of Hollywood's reigning love goddess, Rita Hayworth, who was about to go off in search of her own happiness yet again. For Marilyn it was an opportunity to take advantage of the studio's facilities for star building – free voice lessons, drama lessons, and a co-starring role with Adele Jergens in one of the company's numerous B-features, *Ladies of the Chorus*. She was already too

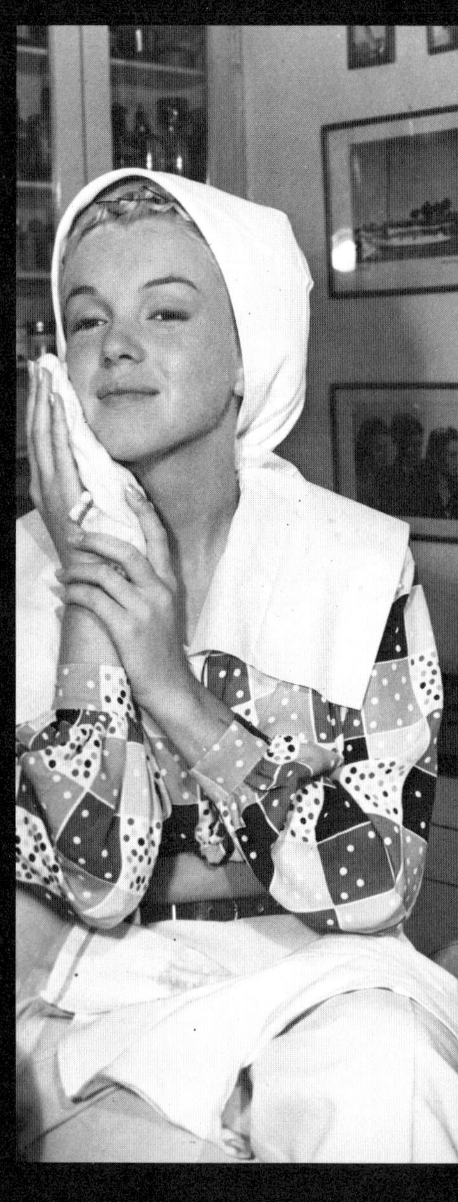

Stages in Marilyn's make-up at Columbia

Ladies of the Chorus. Below: Adele Jergens, Marilyn Monroe. *Opposite:* Marilyn (front centre)

good to be any good in it. Studio boss Harry Cohn's reaction was to drop her without regret. Meanwhile the make-up department had gone to work on her, ignoring her individual beauty so readily discernible when the platinumed and Gilda-styled hairdo was hidden beneath a towel and the face was freed by coldcream from the make-up. They saw her as a cheesecake cutie and wrapped her in a cellophane candyfloss mask that could have been stuck to any one of a hundred faces without causing a stir.

LOS ANGELES
CITY LIMITS
MARILYN MONROE.5

The road to stardom can be a long one, filled with wrong turnings and one way streets. To persevere after having been twice tried and dropped, as Marilyn did, demanded an ambition, a need to succeed, that was greater than Hollywood's ability not to give a damn. But then, she had been born in Los Angeles, had grown up in and around the studios, had read the magazines, heard the stories. In short, she knew exactly what she wanted and knew of the struggle it would take to achieve it, and the countless petty humiliations she would be forced to endure. She was young, pretty and ambitious, and the prize, which she never doubted would be hers, would make it all worthwhile.

Marilyn in 1948

Marilyn in 1950

Like Hayworth and Harlow, and like Clara Bow before them, Marilyn had flesh you felt you could touch when she appeared on the screen. When she stumbled into the office of private eye Groucho Marx in *Love Happy* (1948), as a blonde with a dress too tight and a mouth too loose, and told him with an anxious look 'Some men are following me,' it did not need the customary Groucho leer to emphasize how special she was. Though most prospective employers still saw her as prime ogle flesh, the face in the portrait has begun to develop a look of its own, even if it is not yet the authentic finished Monroe.

Marilyn Monroe, Groucho Marx, *Love Happy*

Marilyn Monroe (right), *Ticket to Tomahawk*

In the chorus of *Ticket to Tomahawk* (1950), an amiable musical set in the Wild West starring Dan Dailey and Anne Baxter, released before *The Asphalt Jungle* and *All About Eve*, she stands out from the rest of the troupe, although the part is little more than scenery. After a mere two years, the girl who had been like millions of others had become the one in a million. Her figure, 38-25-37, had been translated into every language, and each new rival who popped up in her wake had her measurements compared with Marilyn's. Her bright confident smile was seen on billboards and in advertisements for everything in which her studio had an interest. Monthly the glossy magazines vied for attention with articles, photo-spreads and in-depth coverage on her. Nothing could dim her lustre. A publicity man's gag that Marilyn would look good in anything resulted in her posing in a converted potato sack. It was the sort of light-hearted good-humoured lark through which she won ever increasing audiences.

The famous calendar 'Golden Dreams'

In the summer of 1949 Monroe posed nude for photographer Tom Kelley who needed a 'Golden Dream' girl for a calendar. The calendar went on its regular rounds without creating any fuss, and if she had not made good no more would have been heard about it. In 1952, when she was the world's favourite pin-up, the old calendar was dug out for the sort of publicity that might have ruined her hard-won career. She was questioned about it. Why did she do it? 'Hunger.' What did she have on? 'The radio.' Honesty and humour were her unbeatable weapons.

Monroe was also rumoured to have made several soft-core pornographic films like *The Girl, the Coke and the Apple*, from which these frames were taken. Though blurred, one need only look at the eyes and the shape of the eyebrows and compare them with other images of the early Monroe to see the difference.

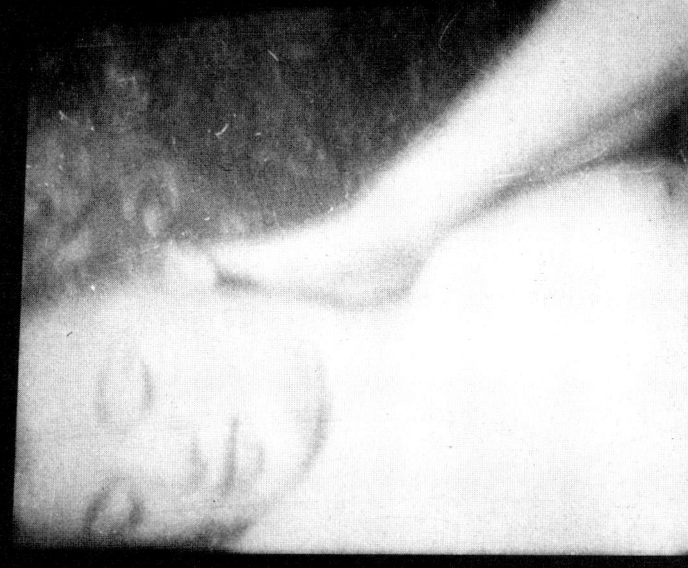

Unidentified stripper – probably Candy Barr – in *The Girl, the Coke and the Apple*, c. 1948

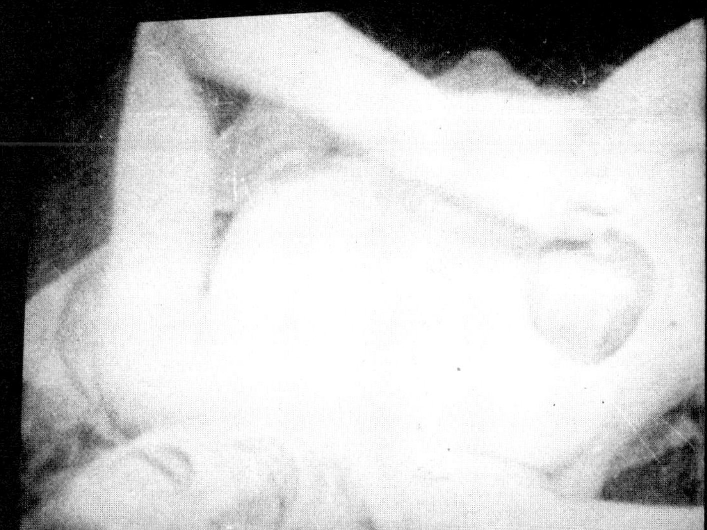

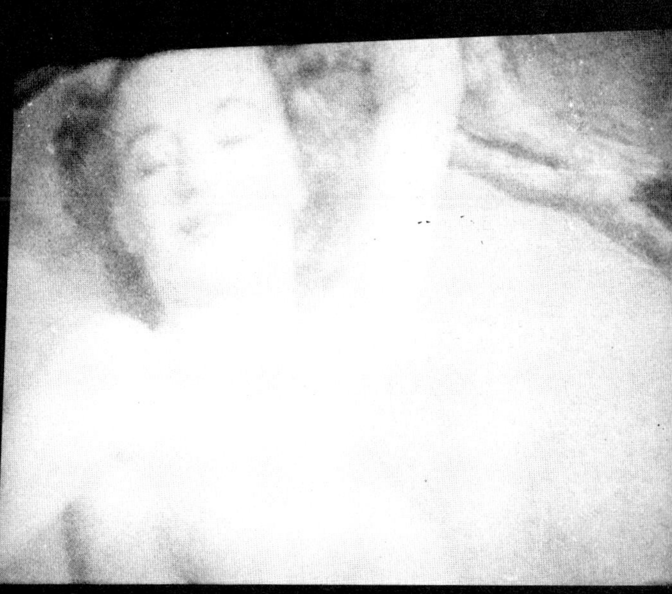

A small-budget film directed by John Huston, who was so important in Hollywood that he was even allowed to make small-budget films, proved to be Marilyn's springboard to fame. Her scenes were few but Huston helped her make them telling. Perhaps he sympathized with her aspirations or was touched by her need for approval. More probably he wanted his film to be all of a piece and for that she must be good.

Because she was the only glamour in a film that avoided it, the promotion for the film concentrated on emphasizing her face and body in all the advertisements. For once audiences, usually annoyed by similar con-tricks to bring them into the cinemas, were not disappointed. The film, *The Asphalt Jungle*, was good, and Marilyn came over well. The starlet with the body became the girl with a face and a name to remember. She was on her way.

Glamour shot, 1950

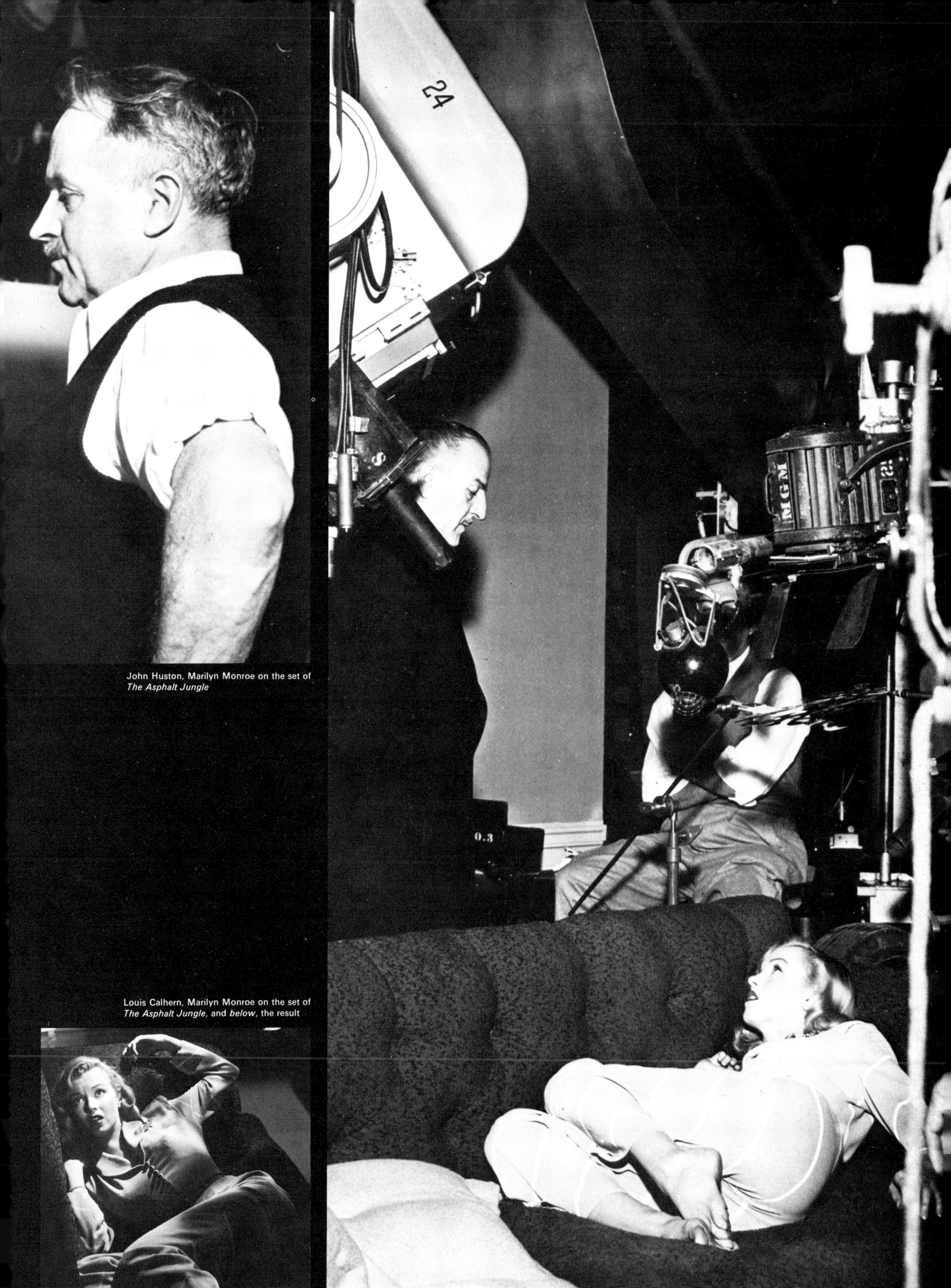

John Huston, Marilyn Monroe on the set of *The Asphalt Jungle*

Louis Calhern, Marilyn Monroe on the set of *The Asphalt Jungle*, and *below*, the result

HOME BUT NOT DRY . . .

Her guileless beauty and unshakeable confidence in her future were qualities to which the camera responded. Her energy commanded attention, particularly among the studio people who make it their business to recognize talent. In company with Bette Davis and George Sanders in the high-powered, prestigious *All About Eve*, she was Miss Caswell, a graduate of the Copacabana School of Dramatic Art – the archetypal piece of 'ogle flesh'. While the high-powered stars prowled through exits and entrances exuding virtuosity, emitting powerful

Marilyn Monroe, James Brown, Mickey Rooney, *The Fireball*

Bette Davis, Marilyn Monroe, George Sanders, *All About Eve*

Dick Powell, Marilyn Monroe, *Right Cross*

lan Hale Jr, Marilyn Monroe, *Home Town Story*

tarlets were expected to provide their own vardrobe. This outfit also served Marilyn in *he Fireball* (see page 58)

Marilyn Monroe, *As Young As You Fee*

charges of personality and xchanging the sharpest dialogue ieard from the screen for a long ime, Marilyn played a pretty girl who said little, pushed no one, and wasn't out to do anybody in. She stood decoratively in a pretty dress and miled disarmingly while the others made asides about her. She was like a tranquil lull in the action. She did not come on as he brash and noisy piece of iightclub glitter the part uggested. She was fresh, and she was noticed.

Marilyn and a cameraman on the set of *Clash by Nigh*

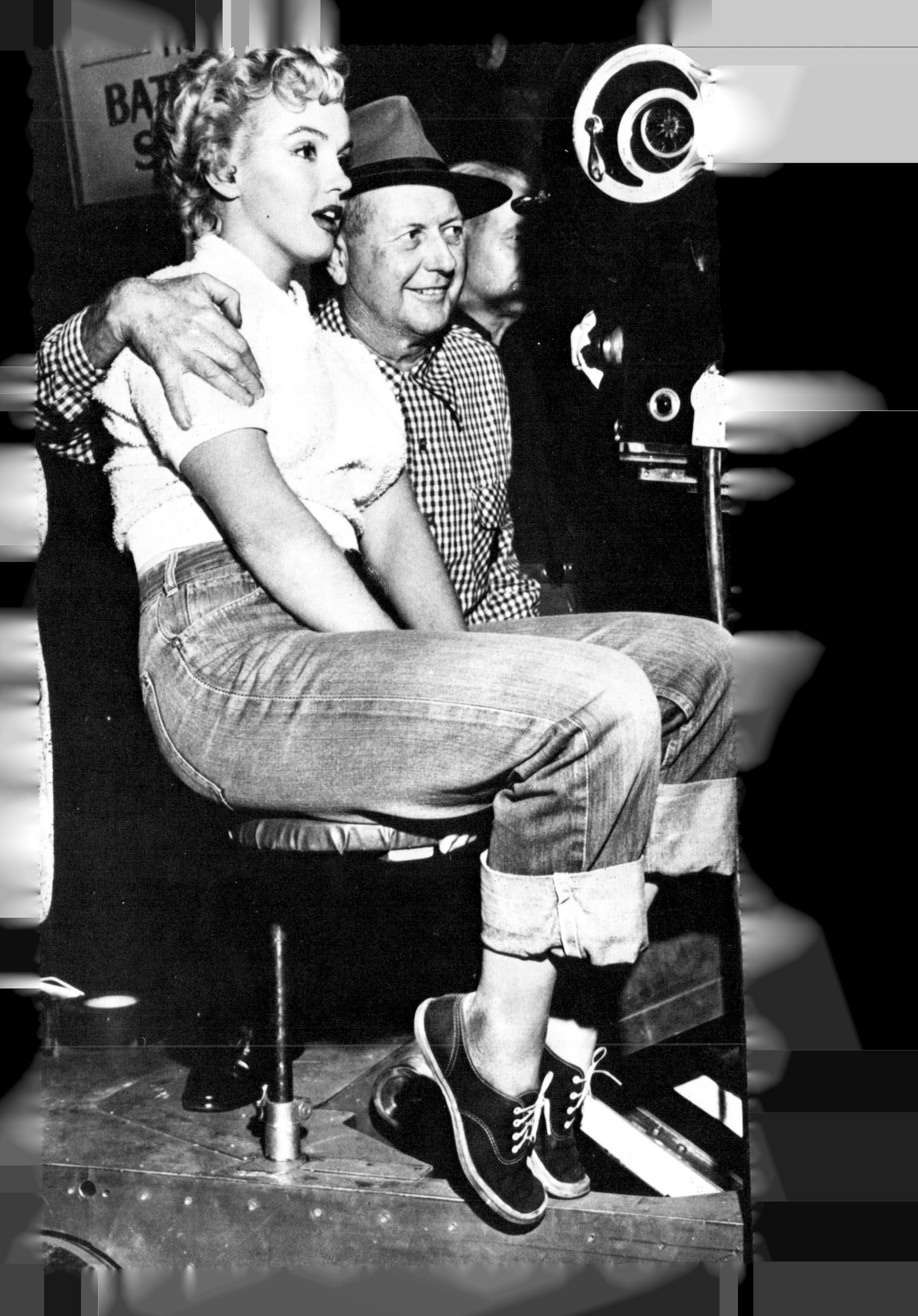

Marilyn Monroe and David Wayne at a party

Marilyn Monroe, David Wayne, *We're Not Married*

Other parts were offered in a steady stream. The studio wanted to benefit from the public's rapidly growing interest in her. A re-issue of *Love Happy* boasted the legend on cinema hoardings: 'with MARILYN MONROE, that girl from *Asphalt Jungle*.' Metro Goldwyn Mayer, who had hesitated in signing her, not wishing to offend their resident blonde star Lana Turner, saw 20th Century Fox sign Marilyn to a seven-year contract in October, 1950. Although at first there was no noticeable improvement in the quality of her roles, she was on the screen for longer and longer. Stardom was only a matter of months away. Now other studios were making offers for her services and

Publicity for *Clash By Night* (*left*), and with Keith Andes in the film (*right*)

Marilyn Monroe, *Don't Bother To Knock*

Marilyn Monroe being directed by Roy Ward Baker in *Don't Bother to Knoc*

one of the few Fox accepted was a significant co-starring role over at RKO – Fritz Lang's *Clash By Night*. She was in prestigious company – Barbara Stanwyck, Paul Douglas and Robert Ryan. Lang, brilliant, professional, was not enthusiastic about the girl whose insecurities in her work created delays. He re-arranged the shooting schedule so no day would begin with any of her scenes. But his star, Barbara Stanwyck, who was not known as 'The Lady' for nothing, told him: 'Don't fool yourself. This girl is a coming star.' She showed neither impatience nor temperament when one of her scenes was repeatedly ruined by Marilyn's difficulty in timing and remembering her few lines.

When the press came on the set, ostensibly to interview Miss Stanwyck, they said, 'We don't want to speak with her. We know everything about her. We want to talk with the girl with the big tits.'* When the film came out Monroe received the attention.

This was the look, provocative, mocking, sensual, which dominated the early 50s and was imitated but never equalled.

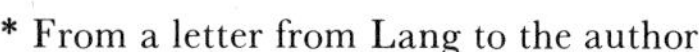

* From a letter from Lang to the author

Early pin-up shots

She was gaining praise as a comedienne, and was loved in and for everything. Having her appendix out was a cause for headlines and a flood of fan-mail. She was now the studio's single most valuable property and earning 750 dollars a week.

Marilyn Monroe, Cary Grant, *Monkey Business*

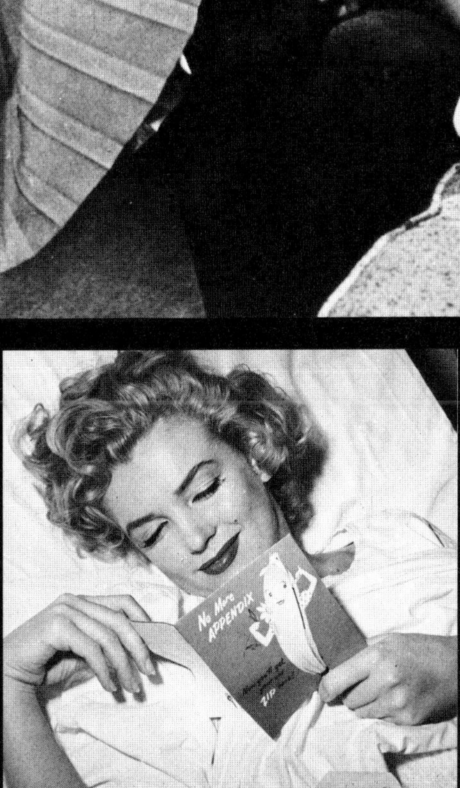

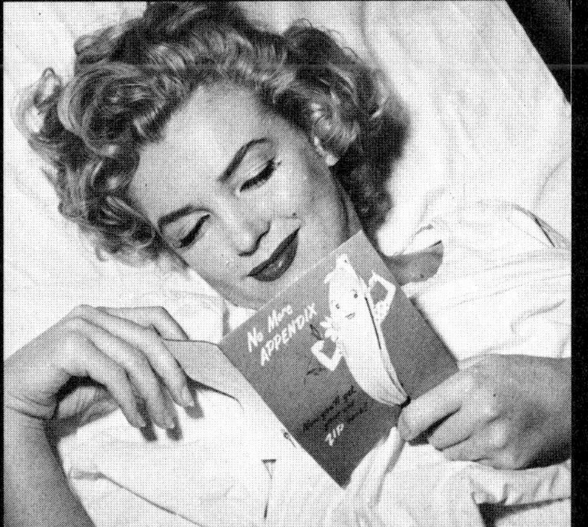

Recovering from the appendix operation

Marilyn, Donald O'Connor

Alan Ladd, Fred Samris, Dick Powell, Marilyn

Paul Douglas, Marilyn

At the year's end she was a regular recipient of awards voting her the public's favourite. She arrived to collect them with escorts the studio lined up for her, and in dresses they loaned her for the occasion. Like Cinderella she would arrive at the studio before the event to be made up and fitted out: the dazzling, recklessly beautiful package was then driven to the party, where photographers had been waiting for just this moment. Overnight she was the brightest star in that whole vanished galaxy. Outraged by what she thought of Marilyn's image when she had

Marilyn at a première

come to accept the Photoplay Gold Medal award as 1952's most popular star, Joan Crawford, a self-made legend in her own right, lashed out in print at her. Marilyn was not taken aback for long. The news was brought to her on the set of her film by a bevy of journalists, who, hoping for fire or tears, asked her what she was planning to do in return. Smilingly she said, 'Turn the other cheek.'

By now, Marilyn's catchy quips were becoming as popular as photos of her. The studio set their publicity folk to start making them up, but the best came from her and were original.

A publicity stunt

Marilyn working on *Niagara*

Niagara was the first of Marilyn's starring films. There was no longer any question of why people went to movies. She was mightier than the dreaded TV. The kind of out and out man-killer she was asked to portray in the film, wearing suits and dresses fitted so tightly as to make every walk a miracle, was not right for Marilyn. As high tension drama it lacked conviction. As quintessential pop art its reputation is ensured by Marilyn seen here posing with the Falls as a less than subtle backdrop for her own charms; for the way-out boldness of her make-up and costumery; and finally, for the 70-foot take of Marilyn walking down a long street in a beige-coloured suit, a modern miracle of the designer's art in that it became like her skin and yet did not split a seam.

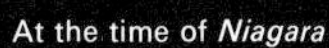

At the time of *Niagara*

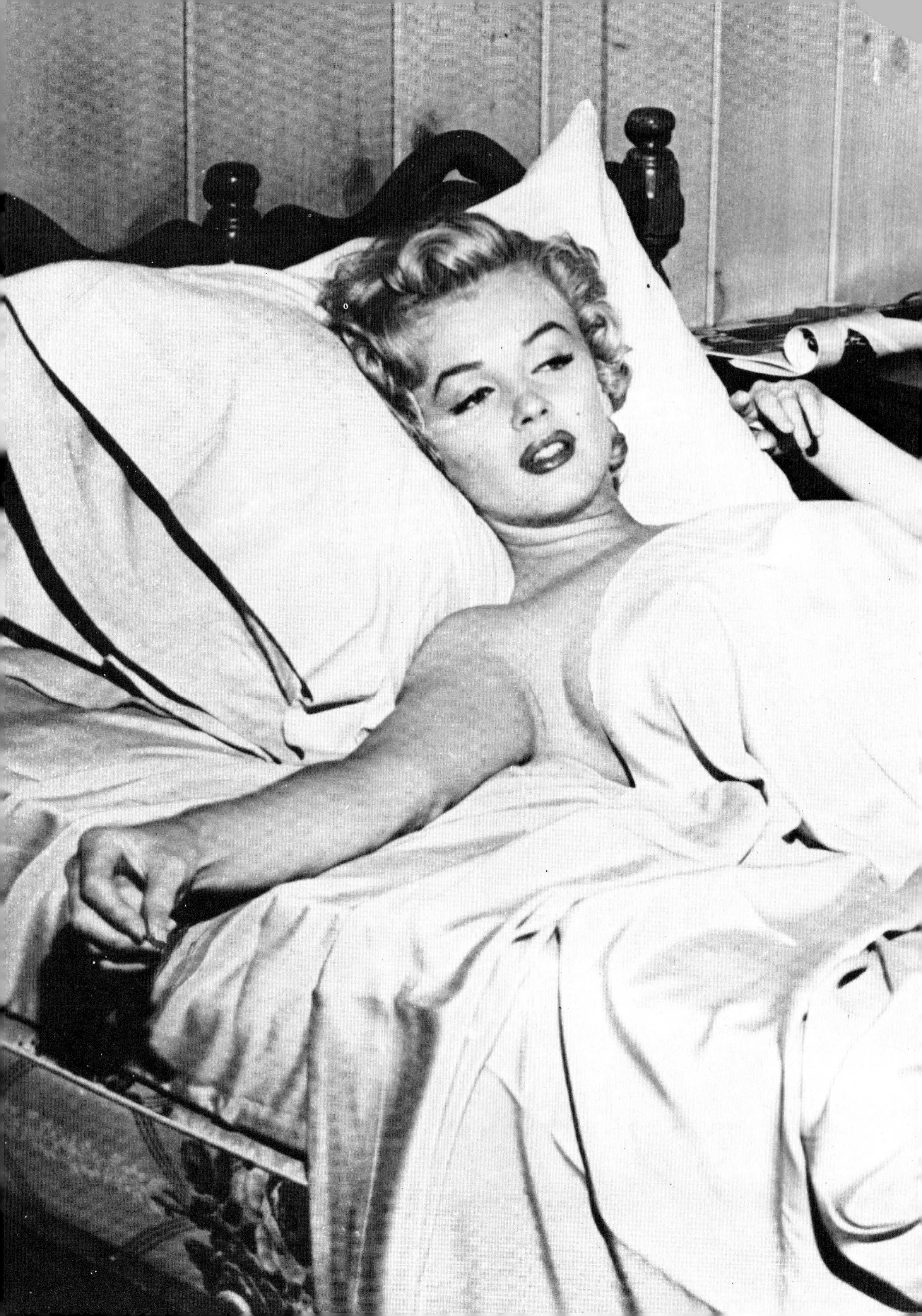

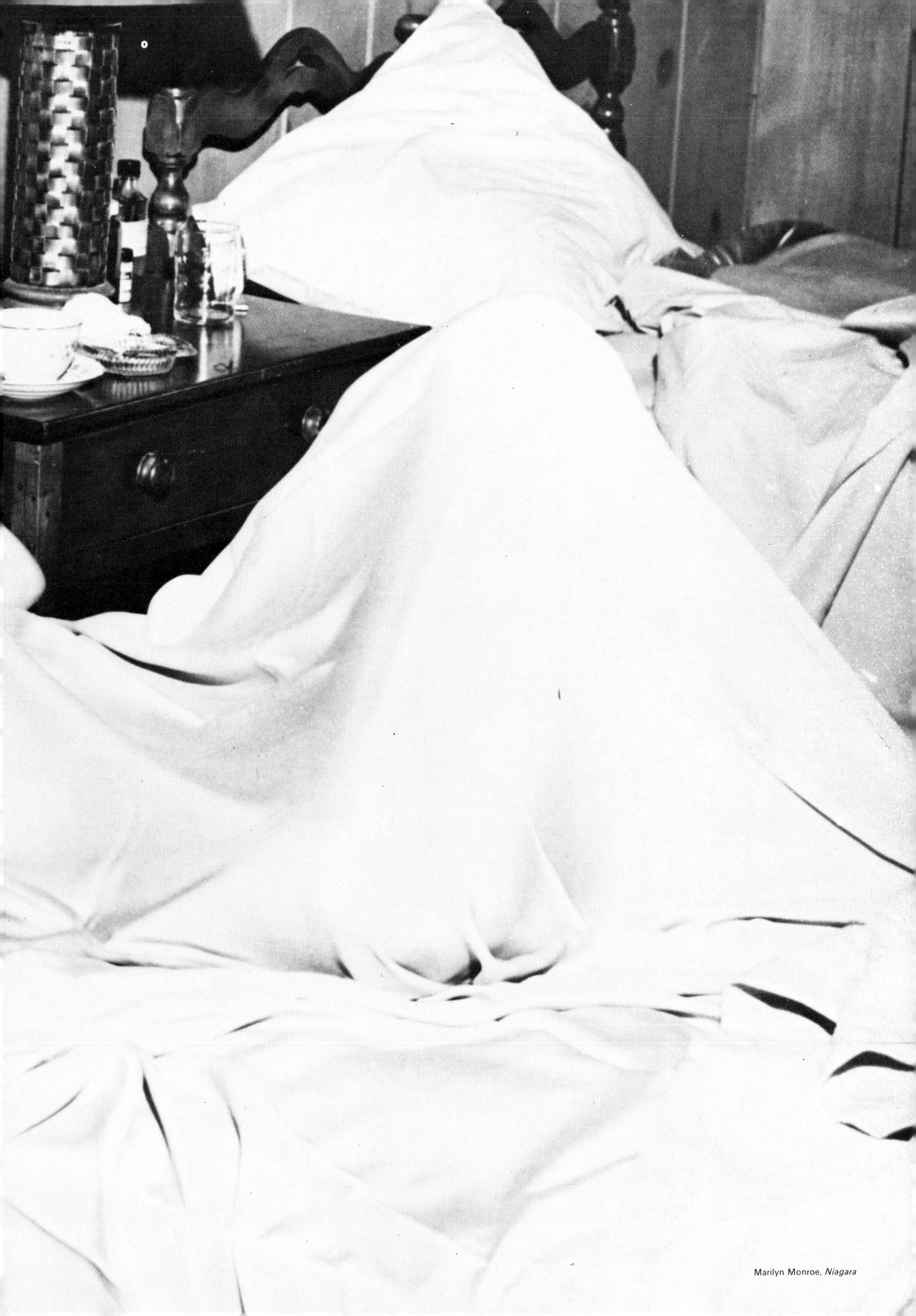

Marilyn Monroe, *Niagara*

Marilyn, Joe DiMaggio, on the set of *Monkey Business*

LET THE GOOD TIMES ROLL . . .

You're a star when you stop looking like all the others and they're all trying to look like you.

Late in 1952 the All-American girl met the All-American boy, baseball great Joe DiMaggio. When he visited her on the set of *Monkey Business* (1952) it started headlines.

Dwight D Eisenhower was the President in America; in England a young Queen was soon to be crowned. The frights and sights of one war had dwindled, thoughts of a new one not yet begun. Things were safe, and on the whole as dull and staid as safe things tend to be.

Marilyn Monroe, Jane Russell, *Gentlemen Prefer Blondes*

But on the horizon was this shining beacon of liberation, Marilyn – Superstar. Her humour, modesty and insecurity had begun to endear her as much to women as to men. They recognized in her a stargazer, acting out fantasies of dressing-up and inviting audiences to share her dreams with her. *Gentlemen Prefer Blondes* marks the climax of the second phase in her career and the beginning of the third. She was home. Not only was she home, she owned the place, and smiling invitingly from the top she seemed to say: 'You see, it is possible. You too

Charles Coburn, Marilyn Monroe, Jane Russell, Norma Varden, Elliot Reid, *Gentlemen Prefer Blondes*

Jane Russell, Marilyn Monroe, *Gentlemen Prefer Blondes*

Marilyn and Jane Russell at Grauman's Chinese Theatre

Walter Winchell, Marilyn and Joe DiMaggio and CinemaScope birthday cake

can make your dreams come true as I have. I've done it. I'm here. Isn't life wonderful!' She was an affirmation of the good things. Now she was fulfilling fantasies faster than she could make them up. Her movies – *How to Marry a Millionaire, River of No Return, There's No Business Like Show Business* – were earning the studio profits which could be directly attributed to her. For when you saw her, you felt good. Good enough in her presence to ignore the dull, dumb plots which she was tiring of. Her efforts to avoid them would soon lead to her suspension; meanwhile she did her utmost to overcome them. She deserved better things than the re-hash of old vehicles that Darryl F Zanuck tended to

Marilyn Monroe, *How to Marry a Millionaire*

Lauren Bacall, Humphrey Bogart and Marilyn at the première of *How to Marry a Millionaire*

provide for the studio's blonde stars. If she hadn't realized this, there were enough hangers-on – agents, lawyers, doctors, drama coaches – to advise her of her best interests, in which lay theirs. That's life. That's being a big movie star. She was the biggest of all.

Nunnally Johnson and Marilyn at the same première

Clark Gable and Marilyn dancing in November 1954

Every country sought its own Monroe – Gina Lollobrigida was Italy's; Martine Carol was France's, and England had Diana Dors. While in Hollywood, a look-alike seemed to pop out of every studio's can of films – Mamie Van Doren, Cleo Moore, Jayne Mansfield, Sheree North, Barbara Nichols, Joy Lansing. These were only a few of them. But imitation is not only a satisfying form of flattery, it offers absolutely no threat.

Marilyn Monroe, Betty Grable, Lauren Bacall demonstrate the CinemaScope ratio in *How to Marry a Millionaire* and, left, relax in the dressing room between shooting

Marilyn Monroe, *River of No Return*

Robert Mitchum and Marilyn in a publicity shot

Marilyn rests on locatio

Marilyn, Otto Preminger on location

Opposite: Marilyn Monroe in torrid costume for an Irving Berlin standard in *There's No Business Like Show Business*

There's No Business Like Show Business was a tribute to the music of Irving Berlin, who visited the set during the shooting of Monroe's big number 'Heat Wave'. Jack Cole, a regular on her films by now, was the choreographer, and Marilyn was developing as one of the most delightful musical comedy stars of the decade. To avoid making films like this one, which she thought a waste of time, she had already experienced suspension troubles with her studio. There were precedents in the lives of earlier love goddesses.

Marilyn Monroe sings 'Heat Wave', *There's No Business Like Show Business*

Irving Berlin and Marilyn on the set

She went on suspension campaigning for better roles (most of her best films were made on loan-out) and for more money. Her salary had not kept pace with her earning power. She knew it, and if the studio would insist on keeping her to the fine print in the contract she had signed when she was eager and grateful enough for any straw, why then, there was always the star's time-honoured method of falling ill in the middle of production and holding up shooting. Naturally the studio tried to make her out to be an ungrateful spoilt child, but the charge did not stick. For one thing, the public knew that it was not the studio who had made Marilyn a star but they. While on suspension, the World's Dream Girl married Joe DiMaggio (on January 14, 1954) and after a brief honeymoon, went on a fast, rousingly successful tour of Korea, entertaining the troops. Her singing, or sometimes her mere presence in a plunging cocktail dress in the freezing cold, drew frantic cheers from the happy GIs. How could the studio claim that she was difficult and hope to find sympathy when she was giving herself so freely and generously? No, the public knew

Marilyn sings to the troops on her Korean tour

Marilyn Monroe, two scenes from *The Seven Year Itch*

that 20th Century Fox was the big bad wolf. It was in the company's interest to get her back to working for them and they capitulated to her demands. One of them was to make the film of the popular Broadway play they had bought for her, *The Seven Year Itch*, which was to be directed by one of Hollywood's ace comedy directors – Billy Wilder. It was to prove to be the apotheosis of the Marilyn audiences had come to love, bringing to a fever pitch the climate of Monroemania that had swept

Victor Moore, Marilyn Monroe, *The Seven Year Itch*

But it was also to prove the beginning of the end of the public image of the happy, uncomplicated Marilyn who had won out against all the odds. Meanwhile, her arrival in New York that September of 1954 created a pandemonium at the airport which anticipated the hysteria of the crazed pop fans to come. Her husband joined her there and from the bright smiles they gave photographers who found them eating out, no one guessed that the marriage was cracking-up.

Tom Ewell, Marilyn Monroe, Robert Strauss in a fantasy sequence cut from *The Seven Year Itch*

Marilyn dining with Joe DiMaggio in 1954

COSTUME

Scenes on location, and from the film *The Seven Year Itch.* Marilyn Monroe, Tom Ewell

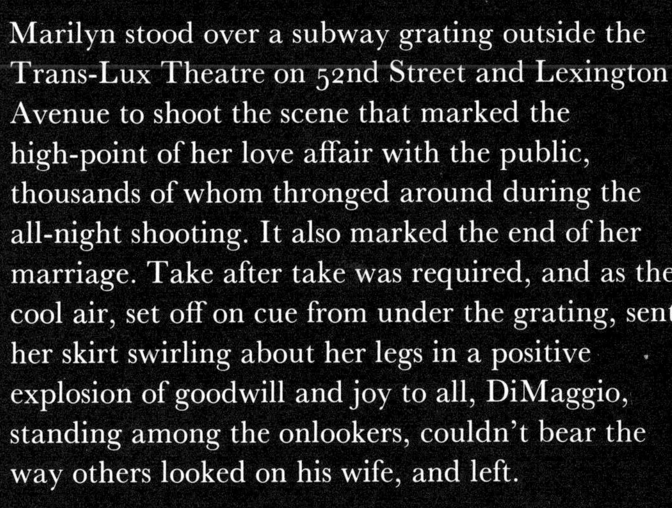

Marilyn stood over a subway grating outside the Trans-Lux Theatre on 52nd Street and Lexington Avenue to shoot the scene that marked the high-point of her love affair with the public, thousands of whom thronged around during the all-night shooting. It also marked the end of her marriage. Take after take was required, and as the cool air, set off on cue from under the grating, sent her skirt swirling about her legs in a positive explosion of goodwill and joy to all, DiMaggio, standing among the onlookers, couldn't bear the way others looked on his wife, and left.

After the completion of the film and the end of her marriage Marilyn escaped to New York; hid in the Actors Studio, threw herself into classes there and helped sell tickets for a benefit performance of *Baby Doll* in aid of the Studio. Spiteful rumours emanated from Hollywood to suggest it was all a

Marilyn Monroe, Tom Ewell, *The Seven Year Itch*

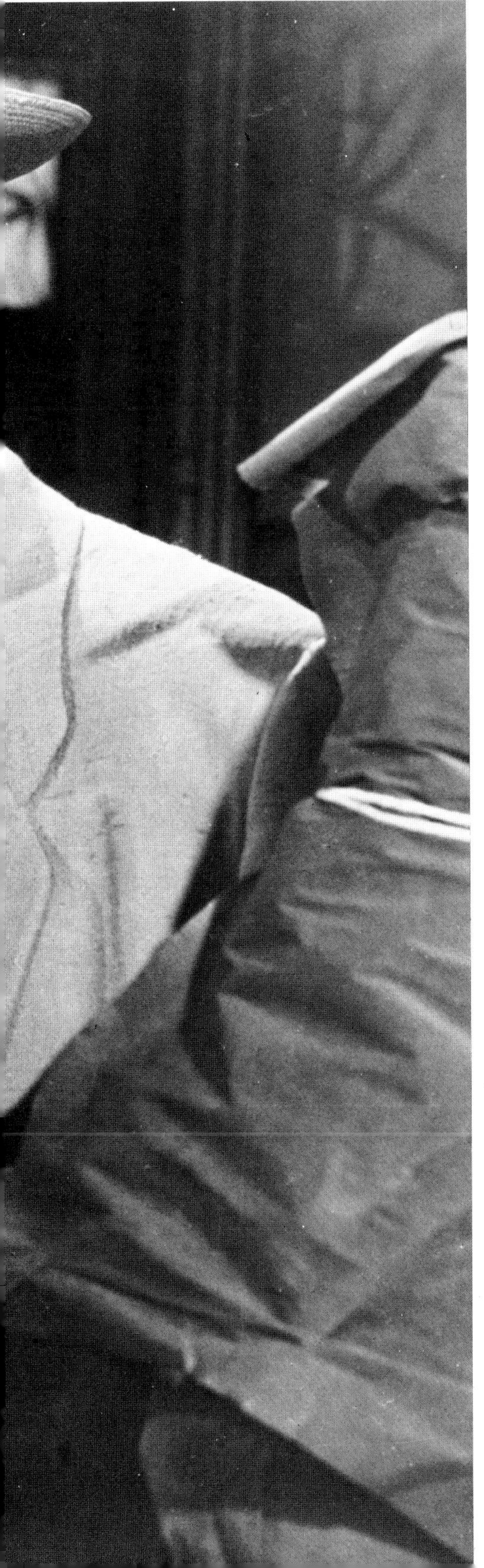

Joe DiMaggio and Marilyn at the première

Marilyn with her attorney after the break-up of her marriage to DiMaggio

ploy. They said that she was not a member of those sacred precincts; and made her entrance into the Actors Studio sound more as if she had tried to break into the Convent of the Sacred Heart to become a nun than into a school for actors. However, word

Marilyn and Josh Logan on the set of *Bus Stop*

soon came from the sacred coven that she was there, personally tutored by the High Priests of Method, Lee Strasberg and his wife Paula. In later years, when Paula Strasberg's presence on the sets of Marilyn's films had become too much for her directors, the sour joke went, 'There's Method in her madness.' That was yet to come. Meanwhile there was Art with a capital A bestowing approval on Monroe's wish to improve herself. After forming her own company with photographer Milton Greene as Vice-President, she returned to her home

Arthur O'Connell, Marilyn Monroe, *Bus Stop*

studio to star in a property specially prepared to her wishes: William Inge's *Bus Stop*. And was it worth it? Was her public still faithful after the year's absence? She played Cherie, the chantoose in a rodeo town who performs nightly to a roomful of loud and drunken cowpokes out for a good time; Cherie, whose dream of success is to own her own mink coat. She ends up in the arms of a lanky cowpoke for whom she is an angel, and as she snuggles against the weather-beaten leather jacket with the rabbity fur collar which he places over her

Don Murray and Marilyn while shooting *Bus Stop*

Eileen Heckart, Marilyn Monroe, *Bus Stop*

Tom Ewell, Marilyn Monroe, *The Seven Year Itch*

Marilyn Monroe, Don Murray, *Bus Stop*

shoulders to keep her warm, the emotion in her gesture says all there is to be said – she has her mink coat.

Alternately puzzled, woe-begone, knowing, conniving, lost, desperate, lonely, confused and unexpectedly radiant with happiness, Marilyn scored her greatest triumph yet. The critics joined the cheering crowds. The intellectuals began to make her their pin-up *and* she had not lost her hold on the public. It was 1956 and she still had no rivals.

Above: Eileen Heckart, Marilyn Monroe and *left:* Marilyn Monroe
Bus Stop

Singing 'That Old Black Magic' to a noisy crowd of cowpokes who couldn't care less about her efforts to entertain them, Cherie is pleased to discover a fan in Bo, the lanky cowpoke who has come to make his fortune at the Rodeo and to find himself an Angel to take back to his ranch. Marilyn and the film were an unqualified triumph. The question now was, 'Where can she go from here?'

Marilyn and Arthur Miller at the wedding

Marilyn accompanying Arthur Miller to Washington where he was to appear before the Senate Investigation Committee

WHERE DO YOU GO FROM HERE?

Arthur Miller, Laurence Olivier and Marilyn at the London press conference to announce the making of *The Prince and the Showgirl*

Laurence Olivier, Marilyn Monroe, *The Prince and the Showgirl*

Laurence Olivier, Marilyn Monroe, *The Prince and the Showgirl*

Laurence Olivier directs Marilyn and Richard Wattis

The first and only film Marilyn made for her own Company was a piece of Ruritanian fluff for which she went to England with her new playwright husband, Arthur Miller. Her co-star and director was the classically trained Laurence Olivier whose failure to appreciate Marilyn's different approach was to lead to a serious rift between them. But the finished product was hers to walk away with.

Marilyn, Arthur Miller at the Royal Film Show, London, 1956

Jack L Warner, Marilyn, Arthur Miller at a New York première

Marilyn Monroe, *Some Like It Hot*

Marilyn signed a contract with Walter of the Mirisch brothers to star in a film for them: *Some Like It Hot*. The director was Billy Wilder. The steam from the train's exhaust creating the longest, hottest wolf whistle was the kind of visual joke he thought up to herald the entrance on the scene of syncopated Sugar (Marilyn Monroe). None of Marilyn's by now famous neuroses were apparent on the screen. Sugar sang, Sugar danced, Sugar secretly swigged whisky from a conveniently hidden hip flask while thinking herself unobserved, and Sugar dodged unknowingly in and out of situations with her 'girl' friends, two male musicians on the run from gangsters in the jazz-aged twenties disguised as female members of an all-girl

Walter Mirisch and Marilyn sign the contract for the film

orchestra. It was all delicious and Sugar was one of Monroe's most loved and lovable creations. It was impossible to believe that any of her scenes were patchwork jobs, and nowhere in any of her scenes with Tony Curtis was the mutual hostility between them apparent. She was plumper and more tender than before, and in some scenes was as breathtakingly beautiful and vulnerable as, by now, only she could be. It was no longer a question of who could act a part better than Marilyn. She *was* the part. It was her presence in the film that made the stag-room-blue Wilder jokes fit for family audiences.

Marilyn Monroe, Tony Curtis, Jack Lemmon in the song 'Runnin' Wild', *Some Like It Hot*

R-145-3

Milton Greene, Marilyn's partner in the Marilyn Monroe Film Co., and Marilyn

Maurice Chevalier and Marilyn on the set of *Some Like It Hot*

Marilyn Monroe, *Bus Stop*

Marilyn had contractual obligations on her four-picture deal with her old studio to fulfil and in the lull before the start of *The Misfits* made a decidedly dull musical for them, *Let's Make Love*. It was the Spring of 1960, and besides Marilyn the film boasted a strong cast including the French music-hall star Yves Montand, the English pop-idol Frankie Vaughan, Tony Randall and others. Director George Cukor was at the helm. But even talents of their calibre could not bring to life a musical comedy that was not funny and had songs that were stunningly banal.

Scenes from *Let's Make Love*. Marilyn Monroe in her number 'My Heart Belongs To Daddy'

Marilyn coached by Dance Director Jack Cole for the film *Let's Make Love*

Meanwhile her relationship with her husband had virtually disintegrated. She was, however, completely the star and aware of the rules of the game, and none of this is apparent in the smiling photos released by the studio to the press to announce the production. But the break-up of the marriage was no secret from their friends or, for that matter, from Hollywood. While Miller went off to New York to work on the screenplay for their joint project *The Misfits*, a commitment too far advanced and too important to both him and Marilyn for

Press conference for *Let's Make Love*. Arthur Miller, Simone Signoret, Yves Montand, Marilyn Monroe, Frankie Vaughan

Yves Montand, Marilyn Monroe, *Let's Make Love*

either to drop, and Yves Montand's wife, the French actress Simone Signoret, had to return to France for an unavoidable prior project, Marilyn fell in love with her romantic leading man, an affair that only added to her personal and now no longer private inner turmoil. Gossip columnists like Hedda Hopper, the bitchy apostles who spread the gospel of glamour in their regular epistles to the faithful, leaked the news of the affair, chiding Marilyn and Montand alternately. Strangely, in the finished film, what sparks there were did not come from the

Director George Cukor (back to camera) discussing a scene with Marilyn

personal chemistry between them, but from the professional one Marilyn had with the brilliant choreographer Jack Cole. While even he could do little with most of the songs, the idea of using a classic standard, Cole Porter's 'My Heart Belongs To Daddy' resulted in one of the most delightful and clever musical numbers to come out of any of Marilyn's films. The film was Marilyn's first failure with her public, even though interest in her and her work had not slackened. On the contrary, few weeks went by when her face was not on the cover of

Marilyn Monroe, Tony Randall, *Let's Make Love*

Marilyn Monroe, Thelma Ritter, *The Misfits*

magazines, or when she was not being written up in the press. Like Hayworth, she was one of those people who attract interest without needing to do anything. Her private life, constantly on the front pages, was fuel to the fire. It would all come together for *The Misfits*. The title and idea came from a short story Miller had written several years before, and on her instigation had shaped into a vehicle for his wife. Neither could then have anticipated how time was to alter them and make it tragically reminiscent of their life and her career.

Arthur Miller and Marilyn Monroe pose during the shooting of *The Misfits*

THE MISFITS

Marilyn on location for *The Misfits*

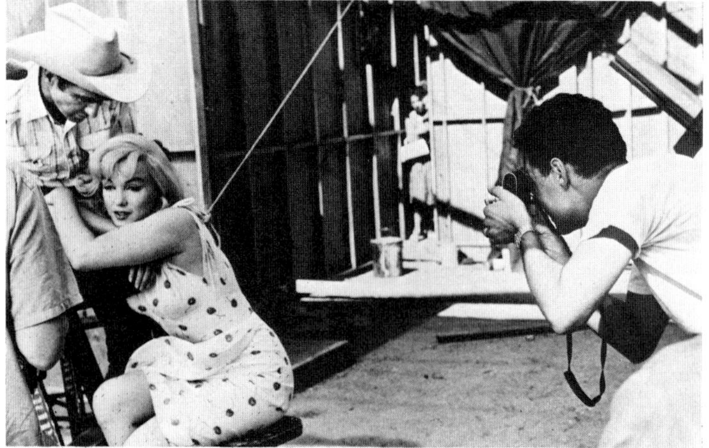

Marilyn and Montgomery Clift pose for a publicity still for *The Misfits*

Marilyn and a crew member's daughter on location for *The Misfits*

In July 1960, *The Misfits* began shooting in Reno, Nevada. John Huston, who had guided Marilyn through her first significant role, helping to launch her on to the career that made her the most loved star in the world, was chosen to be the director for what would prove to be Marilyn's last film. Clark Gable, 'The King', had been on top of Hollywood's totem pole ever since he slugged and loved the screen's great love goddesses in the 30s. He was the star Norma Jean had dreamed about and idolized; the star Marilyn Monroe had danced with

Marilyn being made-up for *The Misfits*

Director John Huston, Marilyn and Clark Gable at a birthday party during the filming of *The Misfits*

in 1954; the actor who hoped that his part in the film would prove a worthy climax to a memorable career, and who died from a heart attack brought on by the exertions imposed during shooting. The screenplay was Arthur Miller's first. It was written as a tribute to his wife, and it marked the end of their marriage.

Eli Wallach, Montgomery Clift, Marilyn Monroe, Clark Gable, *The Misfits*

Clark Gable, Marilyn Monroe, *The Misfits*. The last scene of the last completed film for either star

Marilyn with husband Arthur Miller leaving a New York hospital after she had undergone an operation after a miscarriage in 1961

AFTER HOLLYWOOD CARED . . .

Those whom the Gods love, they destroy. Marilyn went on to begin work on one more film. She seemed to overcome her private problems and encroaching age, to start work on *Something's Got To Give*. She had never looked more beautiful. She seemed, from photographs and tests made for the film, to have become as luminous as the beam of light transferring her image from film to the screen. Her beauty was so fragile, so insubstantial, that it seemed as if like gossamer it would disintegrate at a touch.

Marilyn after her separation from Arthur Miller

Marilyn, Arthur Miller and Eli Wallach on location for *The Misfits*

Photographs by Lawrence Schiller of Marilyn Monroe during the filming of *Something's Got To Give.* Marilyn allowed herself to be photographed nude for the first time since the famous calendar shot fifteen years earlier

Marilyn died from a drug overdose.

Much has been rumoured and conjectured about her death.

Circumstances seemed to make it inevitable. From what one knows about her – the fluctuating moods, the ability to revive and regenerate herself after the various crises of her life (compare the plumpish Marilyn of *Let's Make Love* with the radiant creature of *Something's Got to Give*) – one senses that, whatever else it was, her death could not have been deliberate. For years she had been living on pills. Pills to make

Wardrobe shots taken for the film *Something's Got To Give* which were later used in the composite film *Marilyn* made after her death

Marilyn with ex-husband Joe DiMaggio at a baseball game in 1961

her sleep, pills to wake her, pills to slow her up when she was too stimulated, pills to tone her down, pills to overcome pills. The pills eventually weakened her physical and mental resistance, added to her confusion, slowed down her reflexes in times of stress such as those last days must have been. But planned

Marilyn Monroe, *Something's Got To Give*

George Cukor briefs Marilyn during filming of *Something's Got To Give*

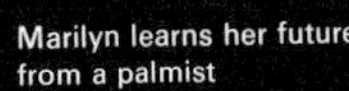

Marilyn learns her future from a palmist

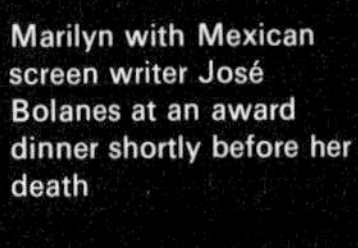

Marilyn with Mexican screen writer José Bolanes at an award dinner shortly before her death

death, the deliberate taking of her own life – that is the one conclusion it would be wrong to make. She stood for Life. She radiated Life. In her smile hope was always present. She glorified in Life, and her death did not mar this final image. She had become a legend in her own time, and in her death took her place among the myths of our century.

Marilyn receives an award for being the world's most popular star: soon afterwards she was dead

The body of Marilyn Monroe arriving at the mortuary, August 5, 1962

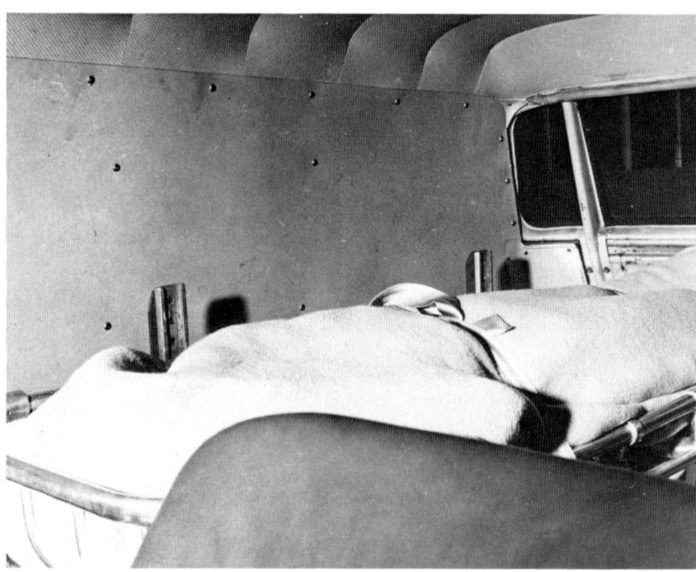

The crowd approaches the crypt in which the body of Marilyn Monroe was interred to pick flower souvenirs from it

Mrs Bernice Miracle (right), Marilyn's half-sister, clinging to the hand of Inez Nelson, Marilyn's friend and business manager, as they arrive at the Westwood Mortuary to arrange for Marilyn's funeral

The casket of Marilyn Monroe being placed on a stand at Westwood Park Memorial Cemetery.
The curtained crypt on the left is Marilyn's last resting place

Dangerous Years

20th CENTURY FOX 9/12/1947

CAST

DANNY JONES	WILLIAM HALOP
DORIS MARTIN	ANN E TODD
WILLY MILLER	SCOTTY BECKETT
WESTON	JEROME COWAN
EVE, A WAITRESS	MARILYN MONROE
BURNS, AN ATTORNEY	RICHARD GAINES
JEFF CARTER	DONALD CURTIS (AND ANNABEL SHAW, DICKIE MOORE)

CREDITS

DIRECTOR	ARTHUR PIERSON
SCREENPLAY AND STORY	ARNOLD BELGARD
DIRECTOR OF PHOTOGRAPHY	BENJAMIN KLINE
MUSIC	RUDY SCHRAGER
EDITOR	FRANK BALRIDGE
PRODUCED BY	SOL WURTZEL

RUNNING TIME 1 HOUR 3 MINS

Donald Curtis, Marilyn

Scudda Hoo! Scudda Hay!

LATER KNOWN AS 'SUMMER LIGHTNING'

20th CENTURY FOX 4/3/1948

CAST

RAD McGILL	JUNE HAVER
SNUG DOMINY	LON McCALLISTER
TONY MAULE	WALTER BRENNAN
JUDITH DOMINY	ANNE REVERE
BEAN McGILL	NATALIE WOOD
STRETCH DOMINY	ROBERT KARNES
MILT DOMINY	HENRY HULL
ROARER McGILL	TOM TULLY
CHES	LEE MACGREGOR
MRS McGILL	GERALDINE WALL
SHERIFF BURSOM	KEN CHRISTY
JUDGE STILLWELL	TOM MOORE
JIM	MATT McHUGH
BARBER	CHARLES WAGENHEIM
DUGAN	HERBERT HEYWOOD
TED	EDWARD GARGAN
ELMER	GUY BEACH
MALONE	G PAT COLLINS
JEFF	CHARLES WOOLF
STABLE HAND	EUGENE JACKSON
GIRL FRIENDS	COLLEEN TOWNSEND MARILYN MONROE

CREDITS

DIRECTED BY	F HUGH HERBERT
PRODUCED BY	WALTER MOROSCO
SCREENPLAY BY	F HUGH HERBERT
FROM A NOVEL BY	GEORGE AGNEW CHAMBERLAIN

COLOUR BY TECHNICOLOR

TECHNICOLOR COLOUR DIRECTOR	NATALIE KALMUS
ASSOCIATE	LEONARD DOSS
DIRECTOR OF PHOTOGRAPHY	ERNEST PALMER, ASC
COSTUMES DESIGNED BY	BONNIE CASHIN
MUSIC	CYRIL MOCKRIDGE
CONDUCTED BY	LIONEL NEWMAN

LENGTH 8,496 FEET
RUNNING TIME 1 HOUR 35 MINS

Ladies of the Chorus

COLUMBIA 1949

CAST

MAY MARTIN	ADELE JERGENS
PEGGY MARTIN	MARILYN MONROE
RANDY CARROLL	RANDY BROOKS
MRS CARROLL	NANA BRYANT
BILLY MACKAY	EDDIE GARR
SALISBURY	STEVEN GERAY
ALAN WAKEFIELD	BILL EDWARDS
BUBBLES LaRUE	MARJORIE HOSHELLE
JOE	FRANK SCANNELL
RIPPLE	DAVE BARRY
RIPPLE JR	ALAN BARRY
TOM LAWSON	MYRON HEALEY
PETER WINTHROP	ROBERT CLARKE
FLOWER SHOP GIRL	GLADYS BLAKE
DOCTOR	EMMETT VOGAN

CREDITS

SCREENPLAY BY	HARRY SAUBER, JOSEPH CAROLE
STORY BY	HARRY SAUBER
DIRECTED BY	PHIL KARLSON
ASSISTANT DIRECTOR	CARTER DeHAVEN
DIRECTOR OF PHOTOGRAPHY	FRANK REDMAN, ASC
FILM EDITOR	RICHARD FANTL
PRODUCTION NUMBERS STAGED BY	JACK BOYLE
MUSICAL SUPERVISOR	FRED KARGER
MUSICAL DIRECTOR	MISCHA BAKALEINIKOFF
SONGS BY	ALLAN ROBERTS, LESTER LEE
UBANGI LOVE SONG BY	BUCK RAM
PRODUCED BY	HARRY A ROMM
COSTUMES	JEAN-LOUIS

RUNNING TIME 61 MINS

Love Happy

UA 10/10/1949

CAST

HARPO	HARPO MARX
FAUSTINO THE GREAT	CHICO MARX
SAM GRUNION	GROUCHO MARX
MAGGIE PHILLIPS	VERA-ELLEN
MADAME EGILICHI	ILONA MASSEY
BUNNY DOLAN	MARION HUTTON
ALPHONSO ZOTTO	RAYMOND BURR
THROCKMORTON	MELVILLE COOPER
MACKINAW	ERIC BLORE
HANNIBAL ZOTO	BRUCE GORDON
GRUNION'S CLIENT	MARILYN MONROE

CREDITS

PRODUCER	LESTER COWAN
PRESENTED BY	MARY PICKFORD
DIRECTOR	DAVID MILLER
SCREENPLAY	FRANK TASHLIN, MAC BENOFF
FROM A STORY BY	HARPO MARX
PHOTOGRAPHY	WILLIAM C MELLOR
EDITING	BASIL WRANGELL, AL JOSEPH
MUSIC	ANN RONELL
ART DIRECTOR	GABRIEL SCOGNAMILLO

RUNNING TIME 85 MINS

Groucho Marx, Marilyn

A Ticket to Tomahawk

20th CENTURY FOX 21/4/1950

CAST

JOHNNY	DAN DAILEY
KIT DODGE JR	ANNE BAXTER
DAKOTA	RORY CALHOUN
TERENCE SWEENY	WALTER BRENNAN
CHUCKITY	CHARLES KEMPER
MADAME ADELAIDE	CONNIE GILCHRIST
SAD EYES	ARTHUR HUNNICUTT
DODGE	WILL WRIGHT
PAWNEE	CHIEF YOWLACHIE
LONG TIME	VICTOR SEN YUNG
DAWSON	MAURITZ HUGO
MAYOR	RAYMOND GREENLEAF
CHARLEY	HARRY CARTER
VELVET FINGERS	HERRY SEYMOUR
BAT	ROBERT ADLER
GILO	LEE MacGREGOR
STATION MASTER	RAYMOND BOND
TRANCOS	CHARLIE STEVENS
CROOKED KNIFE	CHIEF THUNDERCLOUD
ANNIE	MARION MARSHALL
RUBY	JOYCE MACKENZIE
CLARA	MARILYN MONROE
JULIE	BARBARA SMITH
FARGO	JACK ELAM

CREDITS

DIRECTED BY	RICHARD SALE
PRODUCED BY	ROBERT BASSLER
WRITTEN BY	MARY LOOS & RICHARD SALE
COLOUR BY TECHNICOLOR	
MUSIC	CYRIL MOCKRIDGE
MUSICAL DIRECTION	LIONEL NEWMAN
ORCHESTRATION	HERBERT SPENCER, EARLE HAGEN
DIRECTOR OF PHOTOGRAPHY	HARRY JACKSON, ASC
ART DIRECTION	LYLE WHEELER, GEORGE W DAVIS
FILM EDITOR	HARMON JONES
COSTUMES DESIGNED BY	RENE HUBERT
DANCES STAGED BY	KENNY WILLIAMS

RUNNING TIME 1 HOUR 31 MINS

Marion Marshall, Joyce MacKenzie, Dan Dailey, Barbara Smith, Marilyn

The Asphalt Jungle

MGM 5/5/1950

CAST

DIX HANDLEY	STERLING HAYDEN
ALONZO D EMMERICH	LOUIS CALHERN
DOLL CONOVAN	JEAN HAGEN
GUS MINISSI	JAMES WHITMORE
DOC ERWIN	
RIEDENSCHNEIDER	SAM JAFFE
POLICE COMMISSIONER	
HARDY	JOHN McINTIRE
COBBY	MARC LAWRENCE
LT DIETRICH	BARRY KELLY
LOUIS CIAVELLI	ANTHONY CARUSO
MARIA CIAVELLI	TERESA CELLI
ANGELA PHINLAY	MARILYN MONROE
MAY EMMERICH	DOROTHY TREE
BOB BRANNOM	BRAD DEXTER

CREDITS

DIRECTOR	JOHN HUSTON
SCREENPLAY	JOHN HUSTON, BEN MADDOW
FROM A NOVEL BY	W R BURNETT
PHOTOGRAPHY	HAROLD ROSSEN
MUSIC	MIKLOS ROSZA
COSTUMES	HELEN ROSE
EDITOR	GEORGE BOEMLER
ART DIRECTOR	CEDRIC GIBBONS, RANDALL DVELL

RUNNING TIME 112 MINS

The Fireball

20th CENTURY FOX 16/8/1950

CAST

JOHNNY CASAR	MICKEY ROONEY
FATHER O'HARA	PAT O'BRIEN
MARY REEVES	BEVERLY TYLER
MACK MILLER	GLENN CORBETT
ALLAN	JAMES BROWN
POLLY	MARILYN MONROE
NICK	RALPH DUMKE

CREDITS

PRODUCER	BERT FRIEDLOB
DIRECTOR	TAY GARNETT
SCREENPLAY	TAY GARNETT, HORACE McCOY
MUSIC	VICTOR YOUNG
PHOTOGRAPHY	LESTER WHITE
FILM EDITOR	FRANK SULLIVAN
ART DIRECTOR	VAN NEST POLGLASE

LENGTH 7,519 FEET
RUNNING TIME 1 HOUR 24 MINS

All About Eve

20th CENTURY FOX 13/9/1950

CAST

MARGO CHANNING	BETTE DAVIS
EVE HARRINGTON	ANNE BAXTER
ADDISON DE WITT	GEORGE SANDERS
KAREN RICHARDS	CELESTE HOLM
BILL SIMPSON	GARY MERRILL
LLOYD RICHARDS	HUGH MARLOWE
BIRDIE	THELMA RITTER
MISS CASSWELL	MARILYN MONROE
MAX FABIAN	GREGORY RATOFF
PHOEBE	BARBARA BATES
ACTOR	WALTER HAMPDEN
GIRL	RANDY STUART
LEADING MAN	CRAIG HILL
CAPTAIN OF THE WAITERS	STEVE GERAY
STAGE MANAGER	EDDIE FISHER

CREDITS

DIRECTED BY	JOSEPH L MANKIEWICZ
WRITTEN BY	JOSEPH L MANKIEWICZ
BASED ON THE STORY	'THE WISDOM OF EVE' BY MARY ORR
MUSIC	ALFRED NEWMAN
PHOTOGRAPHY	MILTON KRASNER
EDITOR	BARBARA McLEAN
COSTUMES	EDITH HEAD, CHARLES LEMAIRE

RUNNING TIME 128 MINS

Gregory Ratoff, Anne Baxter, Gary Merrill, Marilyn Monroe, George Sanders, Celeste Holm

Right Cross

MGM 22/8/1950

CAST

PAT O'MALLEY	JUNE ALLYSON
RICK GAVERY	DICK POWELL
JOHNNY MONTEREZ	RICARDO MONTALBAN
SEAN O'MALLEY	LIONEL BARRYMORE
MARINA MONTEREZ	TERESA CELLI
TOM BALFORD	TOM POWERS
THIRD REPORTER	KEN TOBEY
GIRL IN CLUB	MARILYN MONROE

CREDITS

DIRECTOR	JOHN STURGES
SCRIPT	CHARLES SCHNEE
PHOTOGRAPHY	NORBERT BRODINE
EDITOR	JAMES E NEWCOM
MUSIC	DAVID RASKIN
COSTUMES	HELEN ROSE

RUNNING TIME 89 MINS

Home Town Story

MGM 14/5/1951

CAST

LAKE WASHBOURNE	JEFFREY LYNN
JOHN McFARLANE	DONALD CRISP
JANICE HUNT	MARJORIE REYNOLDS
SLIM HASKINS	ALAN HALE JR
IRIS MARTIN	MARILYN MONROE
MRS WASHBURN	BARBARA BROWN

CREDITS

DIRECTOR	ARTHUR PIERSON
AUTHOR	ARTHUR PIERSON
SCREENPLAY	ARTHUR PIERSON
PHOTOGRAPHY	LUCIEN ANDRIOT
MUSIC	LOUIS FORBES
EDITOR	WILLIAM CLAXTON

RUNNING TIME 61 MINS

Jeffrey Lynn, Marilyn Monroe

As Young as You Feel

20th CENTURY FOX 13/6/1951

CAST

JOHN HODGES	MONTY WOOLLEY
DELLA HODGES	THELMA RITTER
JOE	DAVID WAYNE
ALICE HODGES	JEAN PETERS
LUCILLE McKINLEY	CONSTANCE BENNETT
HARRIET	MARILYN MONROE
GEORGE HODGES	ALLYN JOSLYN
LOUIS McKINLEY	ALBERT DEKKER
FRANK ERICKSON	CLINTON SUNDBERG
CLEVELAND	MINOR WATSON
CONDUCTOR	LUDWIG STOSSEL
HARPIST	RENIE RIANO
GALLAGHER	WALLY BROWN
WILLIE	RUSTY TAMBLYN
SALTONSTALL	ROGER MOORE

CREDITS

PRODUCED BY	LAMAR TROTTI
DIRECTED BY	HARMON JONES
SCREENPLAY BY	LAMAR TROTTI
BASED ON A STORY BY	PADDY CHAYEFSKY
MUSIC BY	CYRIL MOCKRIDGE
DIRECTOR OF PHOTOGRAPHY	JOE MacDONALD, ASC
ART DIRECTION	LYLE WHEELER, MAURICE RANSFORD
FILM EDITOR	ROBERT SIMPSON
COSTUMES DESIGNED BY	RENIE
MUSICAL DIRECTION	LIONEL NEWMAN

LENGTH 6,906 FEET
RUNNING TIME 1 HOUR 17 MINS

Wally Brown, Marilyn Monroe

Love Nest

20th CENTURY FOX 15/10/1951

CAST

CONNIE SCOTT	JUNE HAVER
JIM SCOTT	WILLIAM LUNDIGAN
CHARLIE PATTERSON	FRANK FAY
ROBERTA STEVENS	MARILYN MONROE
ED FORBES	JACK PAAR
EADIE GAYNOR	LEATRICE JOY
GEORGE THOMPSON	HENRY KULKY
MRS QUIGG	MARIE BLAKE
FLORENCE	PATRICIA MILLER
MRS ARNOLD	MAUDE WALLACE
MR HANSEN	JOE PLOSKI
MRS THOMPSON	MARTHA WENTWORTH
MRS FRAZIER	FAIRE BINNEY
MRS McNAB	CARYL LINCOLN
MR McNAB	MICHAEL ROSS
MR FAIN	BOB JELLISON
POSTMAN	JOHN COSTELLO
MR KNOWLAND	CHARLES CALVERT
DETECTIVE DONOVAN	LEO CLARY
MR CLARK	JACK DALY
MR GRAY	RAY MONTGOMERY
MRS BRADDOCK	FLORENCE AUER
MRS ENGSTRAND	EDNA HOLLAND
MRS HEALY	LIZ SLIFER
GLAZIER	ALVIN HAMMER

CREDITS

PRODUCED BY	JULES BUCK
DIRECTED BY	JOSEPH NEWMAN
SCREENPLAY BY	I A L DIAMOND
BASED ON A NOVEL BY	SCOTT CORBETT
MUSIC	CYRIL MOCKRIDGE
DIRECTOR OF PHOTOGRAPHY	LLOYD AHERN, ASC
ART DIRECTION	LYLE WHEELER
FILM EDITOR	J WATSON WEBB JR, ACE
COSTUMES DESIGNED BY	RENIE
MUSICAL DIRECTION	LIONEL NEWMAN

LENGTH 7,509 FEET
RUNNING TIME 1 HOUR 24 MINS

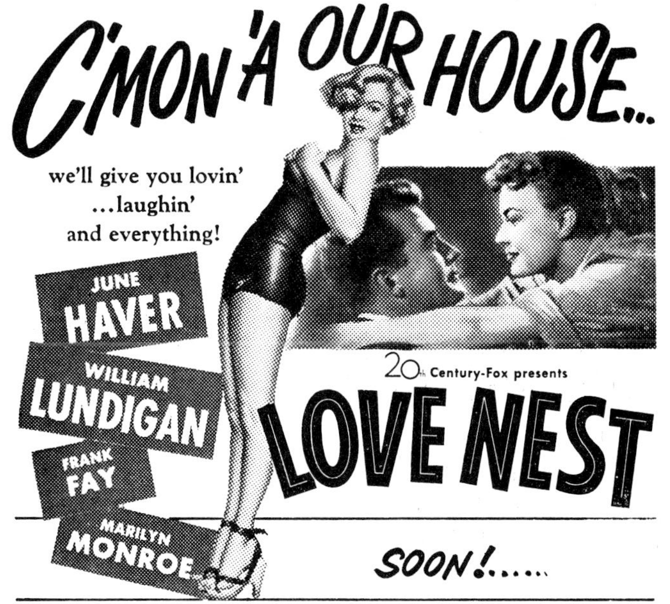

Let's Make it Legal

20th CENTURY FOX 23/10/1951

CAST

MIRIAM	CLAUDETTE COLBERT
HUGH	MacDONALD CAREY
VICTOR	ZACHARY SCOTT
BARBARA DENHAM	BARBARA BATES
JERRY DENHAM	ROBERT WAGNER
JOYCE	MARILYN MONROE
FERGUSON	FRANK CADY
GARDENER	JIM HAYWARD
MISS JESSUP	CAROL SAVAGE
MILKMAN	PAUL GERRITS
SECRETARY	BETTY JANE BOWEN
HUGH'S SECRETARY	VICI RAAF
POLICE LIEUTENANT	RALPH SANFORD
HOTEL MANAGER	HARRY DENNY
POSTMAN	HARRY HARVEY, SNR

CREDITS

PRODUCED BY	ROBERT BASSLER
DIRECTED BY	RICHARD SALE
SCREENPLAY BY	F HUGH HERBERT I A L DIAMOND
BASED ON A STORY BY	MORTIMER BRAUS
MUSIC	CYRIL MOCKRIDGE
DIRECTOR OF PHOTOGRAPHY	LUCIEN BALLARD, ASC
ART DIRECTION	LYLE WHEELER, ALBERT HOGSETT
FILM EDITOR	ROBERT FRITCH, ACE
COSTUMES DESIGNED BY	RENIE
MUSICAL DIRECTION	LIONEL NEWMAN

LENGTH 6,913 FEET
RUNNING TIME 1 HOUR 17 MINS

Clash By Night

RKO 16/5/1952

CAST

MAE	BARBARA STANWYCK
JERRY	PAUL DOUGLAS
EARL	ROBERT RYAN
PEGGY	MARILYN MONROE
UNCLE VINCE	J CARROL NAISH
JOE DOYLE	KEITH ANDERS
PAPA	SILVIO MINCIOTTI

CREDITS

DIRECTOR	FRITZ LANG
SCREENPLAY BY	ALFRED HAYES
FROM PLAY BY	CLIFFORD ODETS
PHOTOGRAPHY	NICHOLAS MUSURACA
MUSIC	ROY WEBB
EDITOR	GEORGE J AMY
SONG	'I HEAR A RHAPSODY' SUNG BY TONY MARTIN
COSTUMES	MICHAEL WOULFE

RUNNING TIME 105 MINS

We're Not Married

20th CENTURY FOX 1/7/1952

CAST

RAMONA	GINGER ROGERS
STEVE GLADWYN	FRED ALLEN
JUSTICE OF THE PEACE	VICTOR MOORE
ANNABEL NORRIS	MARILYN MONROE
JEFF NORRIS	DAVID WAYNE
KATIE WOODRUFF	EVE ARDEN
HECTOR WOODRUFF	PAUL DOUGLAS
WILLIE FISHER	EDDIE BRACKEN
PATSY FISHER	MITZI GAYNOR
FREDDIE MELROSE	LOUIS CALHERN
EVE MELROSE	ZSA ZSA GABOR
DUFFY	JAMES GLEASON
ATTORNEY STONE	PAUL STEWART
MRS BUSH	JANE DARWELL
DETECTIVE MAGNUS	ALAN BRIDGE
RADIO ANNOUNCER	HARRY GOLDER
GOVERNOR BUSH	VICTOR SUTHERLAND
ATTORNEY GENERAL	TOM POWERS
ORGANIST	MAURICE CASS
AUTOGRAPH HOUND	MAUDE WALLACE
IRENE	MARGIE LISZT
MR GRAVES	RICHARD BUCKLEY
TWITCHELL	RALPH DUMKE
PINKY	LEE MARVIN
RUTHIE	MARJORIE WEAVER
POSTMAN	O Z WHITEHEAD
NED	HARRY HARVEY
CHAPLAIN HALL	SELMER JACKSON

CREDITS

PRODUCED BY	NUNNALLY JOHNSON
DIRECTED BY	EDMUND GOULDING
SCREENPLAY BY	NUNNALLY JOHNSON
ADAPTED BY	DWIGHT TAYLOR
FROM A STORY BY	GINA KAUS, JAY DRATLER
MUSIC	CYRIL MOCKRIDGE
DIRECTOR OF PHOTOGRAPHY	LEO TOVER, ASC
ART DIRECTION	LYLE WHEELER, LELAND FULLER
FILM EDITOR	LOUIS LOEFFLER, ACE
COSTUMES DESIGNED BY	ELOIS JENSSEN
MUSICAL DIRECTION	LIONEL NEWMAN

LENGTH 7.690 FEET
RUNNING TIME 1 HOUR 26 MINS

Don't Bother to Knock

20th CENTURY FOX 17/7/1952

CAST

JED TOWERS	RICHARD WIDMARK
NELL	MARILYN MONROE
LYN LESLIE	ANNE BANCROFT
BUNNY	DONNA CORCORAN
ROCHELLE	JEANNE CAGNEY
MRS RUTH JONES	LURENE TUTTLE
EDDIE	ELISHA COOK JR
PETER JONES	JIM BACKUS
MRS BALLEW	VERNA FELTON
BARTENDER	WILLIS B BOUCHEY
MR BALLEW	DON BEDDOE
GIRL PHOTOGRAPHER	GLORIA BLONDELL
MRS McMURDOCK	GRACE HAYLE
PAT	MICHAEL ROSS
MAID	EDA REIS MERIN
LIFTMAN	VICTOR PERRIN
BELL CAPTAIN	DICK COGAN
DOORMAN	ROBERT FOULK
DESK CLERK	OLAN SOULE
TOASTMASTER	EMMETT VOGAN

CREDITS

PRODUCED BY	JULIAN BLAUSTEIN
DIRECTED BY	ROY BAKER
SCREENPLAY BY	DANIEL TARADASH
BASED ON A NOVEL BY	CHARLOTTE ARMSTRONG
MUSICAL DIRECTION	LIONEL NEWMAN
DIRECTOR OF PHOTOGRAPHY	LUCIEN BALLARD, ASC
FILM EDITOR	GEORGE A GITTENS
COSTUMES DESIGNED BY	TRAVILLA

LENGTH 6,846 FEET
RUNNING TIME 1 HOUR 16 MINS

Richard Widmark, Marilyn Monroe

Monkey Business

20th CENTURY FOX 3/9/1952

CAST

BARNABY FULTON	CARY GRANT
EDWINA FULTON	GINGER ROGERS
MR OXLEY	CHARLES COBURN
LOIS LAUREL	MARILYN MONROE
HARVEY ENTWHISTLE	HUGH MARLOWE
SIEGFRIED KITZEL	HENRI LETONDAL
DR ZOLDECK	ROBERT CORNTHWAITE
MR CULVERLY	LARRY KEATING
MRS RHINELANDER	ESTHER DALE
LITTLE INDIAN	GEORGE WINSLOW
PAINTER	HEINE CONKLIN
YALE MAN	GIL STRATTON JR
REPORTER	HARRY CAREY JR

CREDITS

DIRECTOR	HOWARD HAWKS
SCREENPLAY	BEN HECHT, CHARLES LEDERER, I A L DIAMOND
FROM STORY BY	HARRY SEGALL
PHOTOGRAPHY	MILTON KRASNER
EDITOR	WILLIAM B MURPHY
MUSIC	LEIGH HARLINE
COSTUMES	TRAVILLA

RUNNING TIME 97 MINS

O. Henry's Full House

20th CENTURY FOX 26/8/1952

5 short stories narrated by John Steinbeck, Marilyn Monroe appeared in the first of these THE COP AND THE ANTHEM

CAST

SOAPY	CHARLES LAUGHTON
STREETWALKER	MARILYN MONROE
HORACE	DAVID WAYNE

CREDITS

DIRECTOR	HENRY KOSTER
SCREENPLAY	LAMAR TROTTI
PHOTOGRAPHY	LLOYD AHERN
EDITOR	NICK DE MAGGIO
MUSIC	ALFRED NEWMAN

RUNNING TIME 19 MINS

Titles of the other episodes:
The Clarion Call (Director: Henry Hathaway)
The Last Leaf (Director: Jean Negulesco)
The Ransom of the Red Chief (Director: Howard Hawks)
The Gift of the Magi (Director: Henry King)

Marilyn Monroe, Charles Laughton

Niagara

20th CENTURY FOX 22/1/1953

CAST

ROSE LOOMIS	MARILYN MONROE
GEORGE LOOMIS	JOSEPH COTTEN
POLLY CUTLER	JEAN PETERS
RAY CUTLER	CASEY ADAMS
INSPECTOR STARKEY	DENIS O'DEA
PATRICK	RICHARD ALLAN
MR KETTERING	DON WILSON
MRS KETTERING	LURENE TUTTLE
MR QUA	RUSSELL COLLINS
BOATMAN	WILL WRIGHT
DOCTOR	LESTER MATTHEWS
POLICEMAN	CARLETON YOUNG
SAM	SEAN McCLORY
LANDLADY	MINERVA URECAL
WIFE	NINI VARELA
HUSBAND	TOM REYNOLDS
STRAW BOSS	WINFIELD HOENY
CANADIAN CUSTOMS OFFICER	NEIL FITZGERALD
MORRIS	NORMAN McKAY
AMERICAN GUIDE	GENE BAXTER (WESSON)
CARILLON TOWER GUIDE	GEORGE IVES
DETECTIVE	PATRICK O'MOORE

CREDITS

PRODUCED BY	CHARLES BRACKETT
DIRECTED BY	HENRY HATHAWAY
WRITTEN BY	CHARLES BRACKETT, WALTER REISCH AND RICHARD BREEN
MUSIC	SOL KAPLAN
DIRECTOR OF PHOTOGRAPHY	JOE MacDONALD, ASC
ART DIRECTION	LYLE WHEELER, MAURICE RANSFORD
FILM EDITOR	BARBARA McLEAN, ACE
COSTUMES DESIGNED BY	DOROTHY JEAKINS
SPECIAL PHOTOGRAPHIC EFFECTS	RAY KELLOGG
ASSISTANT DIRECTOR	GERD OSWALD

RUNNING TIME 89 MINS

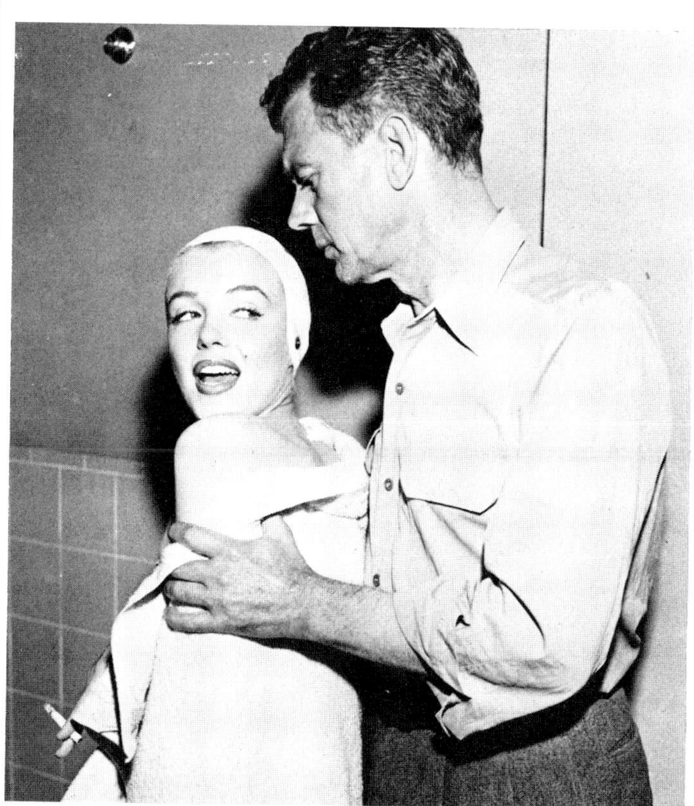

Marilyn Monroe, Joseph Cotton

Gentlemen Prefer Blondes

20th CENTURY FOX 26/6/1953

CAST

DOROTHY	JANE RUSSELL
LORELEI	MARILYN MONROE
SIR FRANCIS BEEKMAN	CHARLES COBURN
MALONE	ELLIOT REID
GUS ESMOND	TOMMY NOONAN
HENRY SPOFFORD III	GEORGE WINSLOW
MAGISTRATE	MARCEL DALIO
ESMOND SR	TAYLOR HOLMES
LADY BEEKMAN	NORMA VARDEN
WATSON	HOWARD WENDELL
HOTEL MANAGER	STEVEN GERAY
GROTIER	HENRI LETONDAL
PHILLIPE	LEO MOSTOVOY
PRITCHARD	ALEX FRAZER
CAB DRIVER	GEORGE DAVIS
HEADWAITER	ALPHONSE MARTELL
COLOURED BOY DANCERS	JIMMIE & FREDDIE MOULTRIE
GENDARMES	JEAN DE BRIAC, GEORGE DEE, PETER CAMLIN
WINSLOW	HARRY CAREY JR

CREDITS

PRODUCED BY	SOL C SIEGEL
DIRECTED BY	HOWARD HAWKS
SCREENPLAY BY	CHARLES LEDERER
BASED ON THE MUSICAL COMEDY BY	JOSEPH FIELDS & ANITA LOOS
MUSIC AND LYRICS BY	JULE STYNE & LEO ROBIN
MUSIC AND LYRICS	'WHEN LOVE GOES WRONG' 'ANYONE HERE FOR LOVE?' BY HOAGY CARMICHAEL & HAROLD ADAMSON
CHOREOGRAPHY BY	JACK COLE
MUSICAL DIRECTION	LIONEL NEWMAN
DIRECTOR OF PHOTOGRAPHY	HARRY J WILD, ASC
ART DIRECTION	LYLE WHEELER, JOSEPH C WRIGHT
FILM EDITOR	HUGH S FOWLER
COSTUMES DESIGNED BY	TRAVILLA
VOCAL DIRECTION	ELIOT DANIEL
ORCHESTRATION	HERBERT SPENCER, EARLE HAGEN, BERNARD MAYERS

RUNNING TIME 1 HOUR 25 MINS

Marilyn Monroe, Jane Russell, Elliot Reid

How to Marry a Millionaire

20th CENTURY FOX 5/11/1953

CAST

LOCO	BETTY GRABLE
POLA	MARILYN MONROE
SCHATZE PAGE	LAUREN BACALL
FREDDIE DENMARK	DAVID WAYNE
EBEN	RORY CALHOUN
TOM BROOKMAN	CAMERON MITCHELL
J STEWARD MERRILL	ALEX D'ARCY
WALDO BREWSTER	FRED CLARK
J D HANLEY	WILLIAM POWELL
BENTON	PERCY HELTON

CREDITS

PRODUCER	NUNNALLY JOHNSON
DIRECTOR	JEAN NEGULESCO
SCREENPLAY	NUNNALLY JOHNSON
BASED ON PLAYS BY	ZOE AKINS 'THE GREEKS HAD A WORD FOR IT'; DALE EUNSOR & KATHERINE ALBERT 'LOCO'
PHOTOGRAPHY (COLOUR)	JOE MacDONALD
EDITOR	LOUIS LOEFFLER
MUSICAL DIRECTION	ALFRED NEWMAN
INCIDENTAL MUSIC	CYRIL MOCKRIDGE
COSTUMES	TRAVILLA

RUNNING TIME 95 MINS

River of No Return

20th CENTURY FOX 23/4/1954

CAST

MATT CALDER	ROBERT MITCHUM
KAY WESTON	MARILYN MONROE
HARRY WESTON	RORY CALHOUN
MARK	TOMMY RETTIG
COLBY	MURVYN VYE
BENSON	DOUGLAS SPENCER
GAMBLER	ED HINTON
BEN	DON BEDDOE
SURREY DRIVER	CLAIRE ANDRE
DEALER AT CRAP TABLE	JACK MATHER
BARBER	EDMUND COBB
TRADER	WILL WRIGHT
DANCER	JARMA LEWIS
YOUNG PUNK	HAL BAYLOR

CREDITS

PRODUCED BY	STANLEY RUBIN
DIRECTED BY	OTTO PREMINGER
SCREENPLAY BY	FRANK FENTON
FROM A STORY BY	LOIUS LANTZ
COLOUR BY TECHNICOLOR	
MUSIC	CYRIL J MOCKRIDGE
MUSICAL DIRECTION	LIONEL NEWMAN
DIRECTOR OF PHOTOGRAPHY	JOSEPH LA SHELLE, ASC
ART DIRECTION	LYLE WHEELER, ADDISON HEHR
SPECIAL PHOTOGRAPHIC EFFECTS	RAY KELLOGG
WARDROBE DIRECTION	CHARLES LE MAIRE
COSTUMES DESIGNED BY	TRAVILLA
VOCAL DIRECTION	KEN DARBY
SONGS	'THE RIVER OF NO RETURN' 'I'M GONNA FILE MY CLAIM' 'ONE SILVER DOLLAR' 'DOWN IN THE MEADOW'
LYRICS	KEN DARBY
MUSIC	LIONEL NEWMAN
CHOREOGRAPHY	JACK COLE

RUNNING TIME 91 MINS

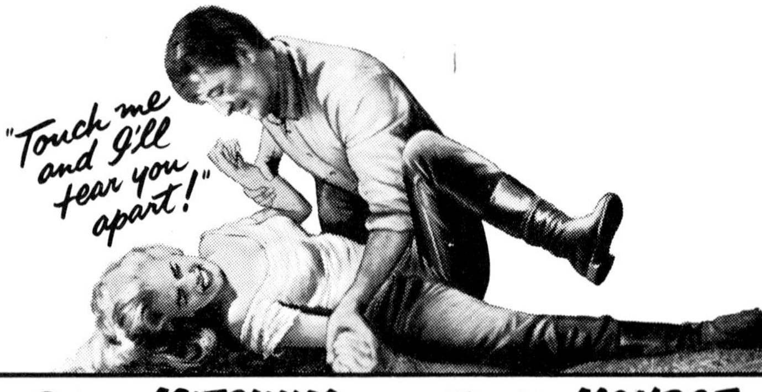

There's No Business Like Show Business

20th CENTURY FOX 8/12/1954

CAST

MOLLY DONAHUE	ETHEL MERMAN
TIM DONAHUE	DONALD O'CONNOR
VICKY	MARILYN MONROE
TERRANCE DONAHUE	DAN DAILEY
STEVE DONAHUE	JOHNNIE RAY
KATY DONAHUE	MITZI GAYNOR
CHARLES GIBBS	HUGH O'BRIAN
EDDIE DUGGAN	FRANK McHUGH
FATHER DINEEN	RHYS WILLIAMS
MARGE	LEE PATRICK
STAGE MANAGER	LYLE TALBOT
LEW HARRIS	RICHARD EASTHAM

CREDITS

DIRECTOR	WALTER LANG
SCREENPLAY	HENRY & PHEOBE EPHRON
FROM A STORY BY	LAMARR TROTT
PHOTOGRAPHY	LEON SHAMROY
EDITOR	ROBERT SIMPSON
COSTUMES	MILES WHITE, BILLY TRAVILLA
CHOREOGRAPHY	ROBERT ALTON, JACK COLE
MUSIC	LIONEL ALFRED NEWMAN
ASSOCIATE	KEN DARBY
SONGS BY	IRVING BERLIN

RUNNING TIME 117 MINS

Marilyn Monroe, Donald O'Connor, Mitzi Gaynor

The Seven Year Itch

20th CENTURY FOX 3/6/1955

CAST

THE GIRL	MARILYN MONROE
RICHARD SHERMAN	TOM EWELL
HELEN SHERMAN	EVELYN KEYES
TOM McKENZIE	SONNY TUFTS
KRUHULIK	ROBERT STRAUSS
DR BRUBAKER	OSCAR HOMOLKA
MISS MORRIS	MARGUERITE CHAPMAN
PLUMBER	VICTOR MOORE
ELAINE	ROXANNE
MR BRADY	DONALD MacBRIDE
MISS FINCH	CAROLYN JONES
GIRL	DOROTHY FORD
RICKY SHERMAN	BUTCH BERNARD
WAITRESS	DORO MERANDO

CREDITS

DIRECTOR	BILLY WILDER
SCREENPLAY	GEORGE AXELROD, BILLY WILDER
FROM THE STAGE PLAY BY	GEORGE AXELROD
PHOTOGRAPHY	MILTON S KRASNER
MUSIC	ALFRED NEWMAN
EDITOR	HUGH S FOWLER
COSTUMES	TRAVILLA

RUNNING TIME 105 MINS

Marilyn Monroe, Tom Ewell

Bus Stop

20th CENTURY FOX 15/8/1956

CAST

CHERIE	MARILYN MONROE
BO	DON MURRAY
VIRGIL	ARTHUR O'CONNELL
GRACE	BETTY FIELD
VERA	EILEEN HECKART
CARL	ROBERT PRAY
ELENA	HOPE LANGE
LIFE REPORTER	CASEY ADAMS
LIFE PHOTOGRAPHER	HANS CONREID
COVER GIRL	GRETA THYSSEN

CREDITS

DIRECTOR	JOSHUA LOGAN
SCREENPLAY BY	GEORGE AXELROD
BASED ON THE PLAY	WILLIAM INGE
PHOTOGRAPHY (COLOUR)	MILTON KRASNER
EDITOR	WILLIAM REYNOLDS
MUSIC	ALFRED NEWMAN, CYRIL MOCKRIDGE
SONG	KEN DARBY
SUNG BY	THE FOUR LADS
COSTUMES	TRAVILLA

RUNNING TIME 94 MINS

Marilyn Monroe, Don Murray

The Prince and the Showgirl

WB 15/5/1957

CAST

THE REGENT	LAURENCE OLIVIER
ELSIE	MARILYN MONROE
THE QUEEN DOWAGER	SYBIL THORNDYKE
NORTHBROOK	RICHARD WATTIS
KING NICHOLAS	JEREMY SPENSER
HOFFMAN	ESMOND KNIGHT
MAJOR DOMO	PAUL HARDWICK
MAUD	ROSAMUND GREENWOOD
THE AMBASSADOR	AUBREY DEXTER
LADY SUNNINGDALE	MAXINE AUDLEY
CALL BOY	HAROLD GOODWIN
VALET WITH VIOLIN	ANDREA MELANDRINOS
MAISIE SPRINGFIELD	JEAN KENT
FANNY	DAPHNE ANDERSON
MAGGIE	GILLIAN OWEN
BETTY	VERA DAY
LOTTIE	MARGOT LISTER
THEATRE-MANAGER	CHARLES VICTOR
THE FOREIGN OFFICE	DAVID HORNE
HEAD VALET	DENNIS EDWARDS
DRESSER	GLADYS HENSON

CREDITS

PRODUCER-DIRECTOR	LAURENCE OLIVIER
AUTHOR-SCRIPTWRITER	TERENCE RATTIGAN
ASSOCIATE DIRECTOR	ANTHONY BUSHELL
PRODUCTION DESIGNER	ROGER FURSE
ART DIRECTOR	CARMEN DILLON
DIRECTOR OF PHOTOGRAPHY	JACK CARDIFF
COSTUME DESIGNER	BEATRICE DAWSON
MUSIC COMPOSER	RICHARD ADDINSELL
MUSICAL DIRECTOR	MUIR MATHIESON
FILM EDITOR	JACK HARRIS
ASSISTANT EDITOR	DESMOND SAUNDERS

RUNNING TIME 117 MINS

Marilyn Monroe, Richard Wattis

Some Like It Hot

UA 25/2/1959

CAST

SUGAR	MARILYN MONROE
JOE	TONY CURTIS
JERRY	JACK LEMMON
SPATS	GEORGE RAFT
MULLIGAN	PAT O'BRIEN
OSGOOD	JOE E BROWN
BONAPARTE	NEHEMIAH PERSOFF
SUE	JOAN SHAWLEE
TOOTHPICK	GEORGE E STONE
PARADISE	EDWARD G ROBINSON
SPAT'S HENCHMEN	MIKE MAZURKI, HARRY WILSON

CREDITS

PRODUCER AND DIRECTOR	BILLY WILDER
ASSOCIATE PRODUCERS	DOANE HARRISON, I A L DIAMOND
SCREENPLAY	BILLY WILDER, I A L DIAMOND
FROM A STORY BY	R THOEREN, M LOGAN
PHOTOGRAPHY	CHARLES LANG JR
MUSIC	ADOLPH DEUTSCH
EDITOR	ARTHUR SCHMIDT
COSTUMES	ORRY-KELLY
SONGS IN FILM INCLUDE	'RUNNIN' WILD' 'I WANNA BE LOVED BY YOU' 'SWEET SUE' 'I'M THRU' WITH LOVE' 'BY THE BEAUTIFUL SEA' 'DOWN AMONG THE SHELTERING PALMS'

RUNNING TIME 121 mins

Let's Make Love

20th CENTURY FOX 24/8/1960

CAST

AMANDA	MARILYN MONROE
JEAN-MARC CLEMENT	YVES MONTAND
TONY DANTON	FRANKIE VAUGHAN
ALEXANDER COFFMAN	TONY RANDALL
JOHN WALES	WILFRED HYDE WHITE
OLIVER BURTON	DAVID BURNS
DAVE KERRY	MICHAEL DAVID
LILY NYLES	MARA LYNN
ABE MILLER	DENNIS KING JR
LAMONT	JOE BESSER
MISS MANNERS	MADGE KENNEDY
JIMMY	RAY FOSTER
YALE	MIKE MASON
COMSTOCK	JOHN CRAVEN
MINISTER	HARRY CHESHIRE

CREDITS

PRODUCED BY	JERRY WALD
DIRECTED BY	GEORGE CUKOR
WRITTEN FOR THE SCREEN BY	NORMAN KRASNA
ADDITIONAL MATERIAL BY	HAL KANTER
MUSIC	LIONEL NEWMAN
WORDS AND MUSIC	SAMMY CAHN, JAMES VAN HEUSEN
SONG	'MY HEART BELONGS TO DADDY' BY COLE PORTER
MUSICAL NUMBERS STAGED BY	JACK COLE
DIRECTOR OF PHOTOGRAPHY	DANIEL L FAPP, ASC
ART DIRECTION	LYLE R WHEELER
FILM EDITOR	DAVID BRETHERTON
COSTUMES DESIGNED BY	DOROTHY JEAKINS

RUNNING TIME 118 mins

The Misfits

UA 1/2/1961

CAST

GAY LANGLAND	CLARK GABLE
ROSLYN TABOR	MARILYN MONROE
PERCE HOWLAND	MONTGOMERY CLIFT
ISABELLE STEERS	THELMA RITTER
GUIDO	ELI WALLACH
THE OLD MAN IN THE BAR	JAMES BARTON
THE CHURCH LADY	ESTELLE WINWOOD
ROSLYN'S HUSBAND, RAYMOND TABER	KEVIN McCARTHY
YOUNG BOY IN BAR	DENNIS SHAW
CHARLES STEERS	PHILIP MITCHELL
OLD GROOM	WALTER RAMAGE
YOUNG BRIDE	PEGGY BARTON
FRESH COWBOY IN BAR	J LEWIS SMITH
SUSAN (AT R.R. STATION)	MARIETTA TREE
BARTENDER	BOBBY LaSALLE
MAN IN BAR	RYALL BOWKER
AMBULANCE ATTENDANT	RALPH ROBERTS

CREDITS

PRODUCED BY	FRANK E TAYLOR
DIRECTED BY	JOHN HUSTON
SCREENPLAY BY	ARTHUR MILLER
MUSIC COMPOSED AND CONDUCTED BY	ALEX NORTH
DIRECTOR OF PHOTOGRAPHY	RUSSELL METTY, ASC
FILM EDITOR	GEORGE TOMASINI, ACE
MAIN TITLES	GEORGE NELSON & CO
COSTUMES	JEAN-LOUIS

RUNNING TIME 2 HOURS 4 MINS

CLARK **Gable** MARILYN **Monroe** MONTGOMERY **Clift**

in the John Huston production

CO-STARRING Thelma Ritter Eli Wallach **the Misfits**

screenplay by Arthur Miller produced by Frank E. Taylor directed by John Huston

Music by Alex North A Seven Arts Productions Presentation Released thru United Artists

Something's Got to Give

20th CENTURY FOX 1962

CAST

MARILYN MONROE
DEAN MARTIN
CYD CHARISSE
PHIL SILVERS
WALLY COX

CREDITS

DIRECTOR	GEORGE CUKOR
SCREENPLAY	WALTER BERNSTEIN
ASSOCIATE PRODUCER & ART DIRECTOR	GENE ALLEN
PRODUCER	HENRY T. WEINSTEIN
PHOTOGRAPHY	FRANZ PLANER
COSTUMES	JEAN-LOUIS

DUE TO MARILYN MONROE'S SUSPENSION AND SUBSEQUENT DEATH, THIS FILM WAS NEVER COMPLETED, AND WAS RE-SHOT WITH DORIS DAY, JAMES GARNER AND POLLY BERGEN IN THE ROLES ORIGINALLY INTENDED FOR MONROE, MARTIN AND CHARISSE IN WHAT WAS A REMAKE OF 'MY FAVOURITE WIFE', AND CALLED 'MOVE OVER DARLING' (1963)

THE LEGEND

BIBLIOGRAPHY

Carpozi, George THE AGONY OF MARILYN MONROE *World Distributors, London, 1962.*

Conway, Michael, *and* Ricci, Mark THE FILMS OF MARILYN MONROE *Citadel Press, New York, 1964.*

Duran, Manuel VIDA Y MUERTE DE UN MITO *Universidad Nacional Autónoma de México, Mexico City, 1965. (Cuadernos de cine no. 13)*

Giglio, Tommaso MARILYN MONROE *Guanda, Bologna, 1956.*

Gilson, René MARILYN MONROE, 1926–1962 *Anthologie du Cinéma, Paris, 1969.*

Goode, James THE STORY OF *THE MISFITS* *Bobbs-Merrill, New York, 1963.*

Guiles, Fred Lawrence NORMA JEAN: THE LIFE OF MARILYN MONROE *McGraw-Hill Book Co., New York, 1969; W H Allen, London, 1969.*

Hoyt, Edwin P MARILYN: THE TRAGIC VENUS *Duell, Sloan & Pearce, New York, 1965.*

Kyrou, Ado MARILYN MONROE *Denoël, Paris, 1972. (Collection étoiles)*

Laclos, Michel MARILYN MONROE *Jean-Jacques Pauvert, Paris, 1963. (Vedettes du cinéma series)*

Madsen, Kai Berg EN AMERIKANSK SUKCES: HISTORIEN OM MARILYN MONROE *Illustrationsforlaget, Copenhagen, 1954.*

Mailer, Norman MARILYN: A BIOGRAPHY *Grosset & Dunlap Inc., New York, 1973; Hodder, London, 1973.*

Martin, Pete WILL ACTING SPOIL MARILYN MONROE? *Doubleday, New York, 1956.*

Smith, Milburn, *and others* MARILYN *Barven Publications, New York, 1971. (Screen Greats Series no. 4)*

Wagenknecht, Edward, *editor* MARILYN MONROE: A COMPOSITE VIEW *Chilton Book Company, Philadelphia, 1969.*

Zolotow, Maurice MARILYN MONROE *W H Allen, London, 1961.*

Axelrod, George & Shaw, Sam MARILYN MONROE AS THE GIRL: The Making of *The Seven Year Itch* in Pictures by Sam Shaw; Foreword by George Axelrod. *Ballantine Books New York, 1955.*

Hamblett, Charles WHO KILLED MARILYN MONROE? or Cage to Catch our Dreams. *Leslie Frewin Ltd., London, 1966.*

Bessie, Alvah THE SYMBOL: a novel whose main heroine bears close study and gives a more penetrating insight into a girl like Marilyn than is usually allowed a biographer. *The Bodley Head, Ltd., London, 1966.*

Miller, Arthur AFTER THE FALL: a play by Monroe's ex-husband whose central character is a self destructive movie star. *Viking Press, New York, 1961.*

Miller, Arthur THE MISFITS: a synthesis of screenplay and novel, including the original short story first published in ESQUIRE which Miller turned into a highly personal movie for his wife, and which he dedicated to Clark Gable. *Dell Publishing Co. Inc. New York, 1957, 1961.*

DISCOGRAPHY

LET'S MAKE LOVE Philips BBL 7414/SBBL 592 (1960). US Columbia CL-1527/CS-8327 (1960).

SOME LIKE IT HOT US United Artists UAL 4030/UAS-5030 (1959). US Ascot UM-13500/US-16500 (1964).

GENTLEMEN PREFER BLONDES (with Jane Russell) US MGM E-208 (10") (1953). Re-issued with 'Till the Clouds Roll By', MGM 2353 067 Select.

THE MISFITS US United Artists UAL-4087/UAS-5087 (1965).

THE SEVEN YEAR ITCH US Decca 8123/8312 Mercury 20154.

MARILYN MONROE Music for Pleasure MFP 1176 (1963). Sound track of film *Marilyn.* Contents: 3 songs *There's No Business Like Show Business*
4 songs *River of No Return*
4 songs *Gentlemen Prefer Blondes* (without Jane Russell)

HOW TO MARRY A MILLIONAIRE One of the tracks on Captain from Castile: classic film scores of Alfred Newman. RCA ARLI 0184 (1973).

INDEX

Page numbers in *italics* refer to illustrations

Acknowledgements

For once there is not a long list of family friends and passers-by to thank for their help in making this book possible. The book was a joy to do because the few who were involved in it shared my feeling for the subject and contributed enormously with their talents and enthusiasm. So thanks, Janice Anderson and Peter Arnold. Thanks, too, Joel Coler at 20th Century Fox for additional stills, and thanks Jeff Fairman for helping so generously. Robin Dodd designed the book so that pictures could say what words failed to, and David Robinson wrote his text with affection and insight, and a beauty which matched his subject. For permission to reproduce the stills in this book I wish to thank the companies that made the films that starred Marilyn Monroe: United Artists, RKO, MGM, Warner Brothers and, of course, 20th Century Fox. I also thank Camera Press, who provided the pictures on pages 144 and 145. The Time and Life covers on page 35 are reproduced by permission of Life Magazine and Time, The Weekly News Magazine, © Time Inc, 1973. The Paris-Match and Neue Illustrierte covers on the same page are reproduced by permission of the publishers.